BULK ORDERS

Requesting a Bulk Orders of this book is easy:

Simply visit our website at:

www.wells2000llc.com\bulk

We offer discounts on orders of 50 copies or more.

Depending on current volume we will respond within 1 Business Day from receipt of your request.
(Response time may increase or decrease depending on the size of the request.)

Please note: Bulk orders are non-returnable.

Military Sexual Trauma

A Brief
Overview

Military Sexual Trauma

www.wells2000.com
www.GIJoan.com

Because of the dynamic nature of the Internet, any Web addresses or links contained in this book may have changed since publication and may no longer be valid.

ISBN-10:   0983706530
ISBN-13:   978-0-9837065-3-3

I thank God, and the Lord and Savior Jesus Christ, for always being there for me.

I thank my husband, Doug, and children, Shante' and Treg, for being my stability.

In Memory of the only one who stood by me then, no matter the threat we faced – my military working dog, "Killer, I will always remember you."

I need to acknowledge Zorro, another Military Working Dog, for attacking his handler when his handler sexually assaulted me. "Thank you Zorro, you deserved better."

To all my brothers and sisters-in-arms, past and present, who have experienced MST, you are always in my prayers.

Author's Introduction

I enlisted into the Air Force in 1987, and became a Security Police Law Enforcement K-9 Handler. My first encounter with sexual harassment/assault was when my civilian shoes stepped onto Lackland AFB. I had not even been in for 24 hours and already I was being targeted. A few months later, my virginity was stolen - I was raped. Throughout the next few years I continued to endure sexual discrimination, sexual harassment and sexual assaults; it seemed to never stop.

I was deployed to Saudi Arabia for Desert Shield/Storm and there my supervisor assaulted me. His own Military Working Dog knew what was happening and attacked him. When I reported the assault I was laughed at and the incident was turned into a joke that Zorro (MWD) did not want to "lose an easy piece." While still in Saudi, I endured the murder of my unborn child, perpetrated by the same supervisor with the collaborated help of the squadron commander.

My enlistment ended with my state-side squadron, 96th Security Police Squadron, Dyess AFB, Texas, threatening that if I spoke to Social Actions I would be discharged. I talked; I was discharged with "General Under Honorable Conditions," and a mental health diagnosis of Adjustment Disorder as though it was "I" that had done something wrong. Unfortunately, my story is not uncommon. Thousands of women and men have suffered, not because of their actions but because a perpetrator chose to assault them, and their military chose to turn their back on and further victimize them.

While writing my memoirs: *Crossing the Blue Code* and *Beyond the Blue Code*, I began to be contacted by many others who had also experienced MST and decided to publish what I had been writing about for years. I knew others were out there who had been silenced and needed something or someone to affirm that what happened actually did, and it was not their fault.

On my own, I have been able to upgrade my discharge to "Honorable." I am now a 100% Service Connected Disabled Combat Veteran, but it took years and help from others to get to this point. I hope this book will be a springboard in educating the masses and helping other MST survivors.

CONTENTS

1
WHAT IS MILITARY SEXUAL TRAUMA?

Rape is the only crime which the victim becomes the accused – Freda Adler

Serving your country by joining the military is an honorable endeavor. There are many positive opportunities, which open up to the individual, such as travel, education, training, and employment. A person can also develop or enhance their personal characteristics of integrity, honor, dedication, perseverance, allegiance, and loyalty to their country, their specific service, their unit, and themselves. Unfortunately, many women and men leave the military with conflicting emotional and physical feelings about their honorable service, such as betrayal, disloyalty, pain, wounds, distrust, and the list continues. The experiences, which these women and men have endured, are horrific, shocking, appalling, awful, repulsive immoral, criminal, and atrocious, yet most were not inflicted by some foreign enemy, but within the very ranks they served, by other military members; their brothers and/or sisters-in-arms.

The conduct of military operations requires members of the Armed Forces to make extraordinary sacrifices, including the ultimate sacrifice, in order to provide for the common defense (AR 600-20, 2008).

MST is an acronym for Military Sexual Trauma; however, deciphering the definition can be complicated. Although sexual assault and sexual harassment have been within the Armed Services from their inception, the term MST is relatively new. The Department of Veterans Affairs, who seemly coined the term, has changed it numerous times and is understandably fickle about its definition when taking everything into account.

Many mistakenly believe that Public Law 102-585 – November, 1992, Sec. 102, defined what military sexual trauma is; it did not. PL 102-585 mandated the VA to begin providing a program for "Counseling to women veterans for sexual trauma."

The confusion started in 1992, when the Bill H.R. 5193, which was designated to amend Chapter 17 of Title 38, was altered prior to becoming law. The Department of Veterans Affairs deals with veterans, and U.S. Title 38 is labeled "Veterans' Benefits;" with the definition of 'veteran' being –

"a person who served in the active military, naval, or air service, and who was discharged or released therefrom under conditions other than dishonorable."

The first part of Public Law 102-585, which is where the mistakes start reads –

"1720D. Counseling to women veterans for sexual trauma

"(a)(1) During the period through December 31, 1995, the Secretary may provide counseling to a women veteran who the Secretary determines requires such counseling to overcome psychological trauma, which in the judgment of a mental health professional employed by the Department, resulted from a physical assault of a sexual nature, battery of a sexual nature, or sexual harassment which occurred while the veteran was serving on active duty."

One would believe that 'sexual trauma' would be defined as it is listed on numerous websites as "psychological trauma resulting from a physical assault of a sexual nature, battery of a sexual nature, or sexual harassment;" however, this is law and unless specifically stated that this is the definition, one cannot just simply make this assumption. Just as someone cannot assume that sexual trauma is defined in this law, or was even in U.S. Code Title 38, neither can it be assumed that MST was defined in them. If this were to be the law which defines Military Sexual Trauma then unless you were a veteran, referring to the above definition of; a woman; required counseling; a professional employed by the Department determined it; and had been on active duty when the experience occurred, then you could not say you had experienced MST.

When Bill H.R. 5193 made its way through Congress; the final draft and end result, Public Law 102-585, removed the definition of 'sexual trauma," which had read -

"(2) The term 'sexual trauma' means the immediate and long-term physical or psychological trauma resulting from rape, sexual

assault, sexual harassment, or other act of sexual violence" (H.R. 5193 – EAS).

With the above in mind, a major missing part of the continued usage of the assumed definitions for "sexual trauma" is the physical aspect; as with the commonly used definition of 'military sexual trauma," left out the physical as well as a whole list of other things. The first title of the code was "Counseling to women veterans for sexual trauma," which would make it understandable for there to only be the "psychological" aspect mentioned. The amendments that continued, until now, never did define sexual trauma. Sexual trauma is not only psychological, and anyone who truly understands sexual traumas would never use such a limiting definition, but the VA did, and continues to utilize it. In a VHA directive (2010-033), Military Sexual Trauma (MST) Programing, it reads –

"MST is defined as "psychological trauma, which in the judgment of a mental health professional employed by the Department, resulted from a physical assault of a sexual nature, battery of a sexual nature, or sexual harassment which occurred while the Veteran was serving on active duty or active duty for training."

This definition again limits the trauma to only being psychological, and further adds (what is listed in U.S.C. 1720D) that a mental health professional employed by the Department must state that the two are linked. If one is to utilize this definition as stated, parts cannot be pulled out, and a person is limited to defining it exactly as it was written.

In the beginning, the program counseling to women veterans for sexual trauma, was:
- optional, not required;
- designated counseling only for women veterans,
- who in the judgment of a mental health professional employed by the Department required counseling;
- until December 31, 1995;
- may be provide fee-based (contract out) till December 31, 1994;

- veteran must seek counseling within two years after the veteran's discharge;
- and not to exceed one year.

The Public Law ended up being 38 USC 1720D and has continually been amended over the years.

Thankfully, the definition of sexual harassment was still included -
"(e) In this section the term 'sexual harassment' means repeated, unsolicited verbal or physical contact of a sexual nature which is threatening in character" (PL 102-585, 1992).

On the VA's website, the latest official definition of MST (Apr, 2015) reads,
"The Secretary shall operate a program under which the Secretary provides counseling and appropriate care and services to veterans who the Secretary determines require such counseling and care and services to overcome psychological trauma, which in the judgment of a mental health professional employed by the Department, resulted from a physical assault of a sexual nature, battery of a sexual nature, or sexual harassment which occurred while the Veteran was serving on active duty, active duty for training, or inactive duty training."

In some of the definitions, of MST, the VA removes the criteria *"which in the judgment of a mental health professional employed by the Department"* (incorrectly listed on several pages on their own site and continually copied to other sites - *"which in the judgment of a VA mental health professional"*) and broadly defines MST as -

- *"experiences of sexual assault or repeated, threatening acts of sexual harassment* (ptsd.va.gov/public, 2014).*"*
- *"Sexual trauma experienced while on activity duty in the military"* (va.gov/healthbenefits/resources, 2014).
- *"sexual harassment that is threatening in character or physical assault of a sexual nature that occurred while the victim was in the military, regardless of geographic location of the trauma, gender of victim, or the relationship to the perpetrator"* (DVA Independent Study Course, Jan 2004).

4

- *"repeated sexual harassment or sexual assault during their military service"* (va.gov/healthbenefits/apply, 2014).
- *"psychology trauma resulting from a physical assault or battery of a sexual nature or from sexual harassment that occurred while the Veteran was on active duty, or Active Duty for Training (ADUTRA)"* (va.gov/healthbenefits/acess. 2014).
- *"sexual harassment that is life threatening or physical assault of a sexual nature. These traumas occur when a person is in the military. The location, genders of the people involved, and their relationship do not matter"* (veteranshealthlibrary, 2014).
- *"experience sexual harassment or sexual assault during their military service. VA refers to these experiences as military sexual trauma, or MST"* (womenshealth.va.gov, 2014).
- *"MST is the term the Department of Veterans Affairs (VA) uses to refer to sexual assault or sexual harassment that occurred while the Veteran was in the military"* (myhealth.va.gov).
- *"Military sexual trauma, or MST, is the term used by VA to refer to experiences of sexual assault or repeated, threatening sexual harassment that a Veteran experienced during his or her military service"* (ptsd.va.gov/public, 2015).

With all these different definitions and their continual changes of official definitions within the VA system itself, there is an understandable confusion over what is and what is not MST. Public Law previously did not define the term, U.S. Code: Title 38 – Veterans' Benefits also does not, and the VA continued to waver on the definition depending on laws set forth from Congress. H.R. 3230, Veterans Access, Choice, and Accountability Act of 2014 has changed some of the confusion as it pertains to counseling services within the VA system. This Act, under reports for military sexual trauma, defines military sexual trauma for the section, as: "The term *"military sexual trauma"* means psychological trauma, which in the judgement of a mental health professional employed by the Department, resulted from a physical assault of a sexual nature, battery of a sexual nature, or sexual harassment which occurred while the veteran was serving on active duty, active duty for training, or inactive duty training" (113th Congress, 2013-2014). This Act also allows the Secretary of Veterans Affairs to define "sexual trauma" for the purposes of that section.

Some would automatically state then we have a definition of military sexual trauma defined by law, I do not agree. The definition falls under the section for reporting, not for the counseling of. To many this can seem like splitting hairs; however, the term has now become a part of the culture, and there needs to be a decisive definition which is not added to here and there for political agendas, counseling programs, and care access. The first of the difficulties is that the VA need not to be defining the term, nor public law. The Veterans Administration is just that, veterans, and you do not have to be a veteran to experience MST, as someone who is still on active duty can have experienced MST without being discharged, which would give them the veteran status. The limiting definition of the term veteran from the VA also excludes persons who were discharged with a dishonorable discharge. Although they continually carry this noose over their heads, they could have experienced MST. In all my writings I have never limited MST to only women, to only being psychological, for any mental health professional to be the judge of whether or not it was experienced, or to a veteran, who was or was not discharged dishonorably; however, there are uniquenesses which do limit the extent of the definition.

The first part is in the term itself, military; because of the factors which cause the higher risks of long-term, more severe, numerous symptomologies, the term must be limited to active duty in the Armed Forces. One of these factors is the inability to just walk away. If the individual can just move on, as if it was a civilian job, no matter the financial or career implications, then that would not be included in active duty determination. Active duty as to being full-time active duty, for training or otherwise. It also does not extend to other services of the Department of Defense, it is limited to the Air Force, Army, Navy, Marine Corps and Coast Guard. Although the VA has continued to expand access to counseling services and care for sexual trauma; that expansion need not include the designation of experiencing MST. As this book will further illuminate most of the distinctive circumstances framing the conditions under which MST occurs, it should become transparent the reasons behind the constraints.

The definition of Military Sexual Trauma is the experience of sexual assault, or sexual harassment, resulting in an immediate or long-term, physical or psychological injury, which occurred while the person was on active duty in the US Armed Forces.

Sexual harassment for the usage above is repeated, unsolicited verbal or physical contact of a sexual nature which is threatening in character. The definition does not diminish sexual assault and sexual harassment which is not MST, just defines it. The continual broadening of the definition lowers the efficacy of the research with the unique conditions MST encompasses and reduces its significance as a distinctive category. It needs to be noted that a person cannot merely have MST. Because it is not a disease (physically or mentally) or a diagnosis; it can only be experienced. Just as a person does not have sexual assault, they experience sexual assault. As the VA website reinforces "It is important to remember that MST is an experience. It is not a diagnosis or a mental health condition in and of itself" (ptsd.va.gov).

All sexual traumas, civilian or military are horrific experiences, but military personnel have circumstances that do not pertain to civilian survivors, and other aspects which are rarely seen in the civilian population. These unique aspects pertaining to MST are some reasons a survivor would not tell anyone about the trauma and likely the reason for a significantly greater number of MST survivors developing mental health issues; generally PTSD, Posttraumatic Stress Disorder.

Military Sexual Trauma can occur: during war or peace; to men or women; to enlisted personnel or officers; active duty, reserve or guard, while on active duty; during training, deployment, Temporary Duty Assignment, or Permanent Duty Station; to any grade; any age; and within any military.

Sexual Assault is defined as any sexual activity between two or more people in which one of the persons is involved against her or his will. Sexual Assault is not limited to rape only, but does involve physical contact. The sexual activity involved in the assault can include many different experiences. Sexual Assault includes rape, inappropriate sexual contact, unwanted touching (such as but not limited to: fondling, grabbing, poking), anal sex, oral sex, sexual penetration with an object, and/or sexual intercourse.

"Military Definition of Sexual Assault
In the Department, the term "sexual assault" does not refer to one specific crime; rather, it encompasses a range of sex crimes that represent a broad spectrum of offenses from rape to nonconsensual sodomy to wrongful sexual contact as well as attempts to commit these offenses. Consequently, the definition of sexual assault in the military is broader than the crime of rape. In its current form, DoDD 6495.01 defines sexual assault as follows:
Intentional sexual contact characterized by use of force, threats, intimidation, or abuse of authority or when the victim does not or cannot consent. The term includes a broad category of sexual offenses consisting of the following specific UCMJ offenses: rape, sexual assault, aggravated sexual contact; abusive sexual contact, nonconsensual sodomy (forced oral or anal sex), or attempts to commit these acts" (DoD Annual Report, FY2013).

Uniform Code of Military Justice (UCMJ), Article 120—Rape and sexual assault generally
   (a) Rape. Any person subject to this chapter who commits a sexual act upon another person by—
   (1) using unlawful force against that other person;
   (2) using force causing or likely to cause death or grievous bodily harm to any person;
   (3) threatening or placing that other person in fear that any person will be subjected to death, grievous bodily harm, or kidnapping;
   (4) first rendering that other person unconscious; or
   (5) administering to that other person by force or threat of force, or without the knowledge or consent of that person, a drug, intoxicant, or other similar substance and thereby substantially impairing the ability of that other person to appraise or control conduct;
is guilty of rape and shall be punished as a court-martial may direct.

   (b) Sexual Assault. Any person subject to this chapter who—
   (1) commits a sexual act upon another person by—

(A) threatening or placing that other person in fear;

(B) causing bodily harm to that other person;

(C) making a fraudulent representation that the sexual act serves a professional purpose; or

(D) inducing a belief by any artifice, pretense, or concealment that the person is another person;

(2) commits a sexual act upon another person when the person knows or reasonably should know that the other person is asleep, unconscious, or otherwise unaware that the sexual act is occurring; or

(3) commits a sexual act upon another person when the other person is incapable of consenting to the sexual act due to—

(A) impairment by any drug, intoxicant, or other similar substance, and that condition is known or reasonably should be known by the person; or

(B) a mental disease or defect, or physical disability, and that condition is known or reasonably should be known by the person;

is guilty of sexual assault and shall be punished as a court-martial may direct.

(c) Aggravated Sexual Contact. Any person subject to this chapter who commits or causes sexual contact upon or by another person, if to do so would violate subsection (a) (rape) had the sexual contact been a sexual act, is guilty of aggravated sexual contact and shall be punished as a court-martial may direct.

(d) Abusive Sexual Contact. Any person subject to this chapter who commits or causes sexual contact upon or by another person, if to do so would violate subsection (b) (sexual assault) had the sexual contact been a sexual act, is guilty of abusive sexual contact and shall be punished as a court-martial may direct.

(2) Sexual contact. The term 'sexual contact' means—

(A) touching, or causing another person to touch, either directly or through the clothing, the genitalia, anus, groin, breast, inner thigh, or buttocks of any person, with an intent to abuse, humiliate, or degrade any person; or

(B) any touching, or causing another person to touch, either directly or through the clothing, any body part of any person, if done with an intent to arouse or gratify the sexual desire of any person.

Touching may be accomplished by any part of the body.

(3) Bodily harm. The term 'bodily harm' means any offensive touching of another, however slight, including any nonconsensual sexual act or nonconsensual sexual contact.

(4) Grievous bodily harm. The term 'grievous bodily harm' means serious bodily injury. It includes fractured or dislocated bones, deep cuts, torn members of the body, serious damage to internal organs, and other severe bodily injuries. It does not include minor injuries such as a black eye or a bloody nose.

(8) Consent.

(A) The term 'consent' means a freely given agreement to the conduct at issue by a competent person. An expression of lack of consent through words or conduct means there is no consent. Lack of verbal or physical resistance or submission resulting from the use of force, threat of force, or placing another person in fear does not constitute consent. A current or previous dating or social or sexual relationship by itself or the manner of dress of the person involved with the accused in the conduct at issue shall not constitute consent.

(B) A sleeping, unconscious, or incompetent person cannot consent. A person cannot consent to force causing or likely to cause death or grievous bodily harm or to being rendered unconscious. A person cannot consent while under threat or fear or under the circumstances described in subparagraph (C) or (D) of subsection (b)(1).

(C) Lack of consent may be inferred based on the circumstances of the offense. All the surrounding circumstances are to be considered in determining whether a person gave consent, or whether a person did not resist or ceased to resist only because of another person's actions (UCMJ, 2015).

Sexual Harassment is a form of gender discrimination that involves requests for sexual favors, unwelcome sexual advances, and other verbal or physical contact of a sexual nature. There are two types of sexual harassment; they are Hostile Environment and Quid Pro Quo. **Hostile Environment** occurs when unwanted, insulting and uninvited behavior happens to a person and it disrupts the work place and the person's work performance. It can create a hostile, intimidating or offensive work environment. **Quid pro quo** is when there are conditions placed on a person's employment for the exchange of sexual favors, and usually entails threats if the person does not comply.

There are many myths regarding sexual assault and sexual harassment. Assumptive world theory supplies reasons as to why the victim is often blamed. These false reasons are a person's rationalization towards sexual assaults by assigning some type of blame to the victim so that the bystander creates for her/himself a false sense of safety. The illusion is if they avoid that particular thing, which they see the victim has done, they will not be assaulted. Most would like to view the world as just and that we have a sense of control. By placing blame on the victim, we keep the myth of "bad things happen to bad people" and "it could never happen to me" firmly intertwined in our overestimation of the likelihood of encountering positive outcomes in life. This also creates an Us (non-victims) vs. Them (victims) mentality which further alienates the victims.

Another misconception is the characteristics of the assailant. When questioned to describe a person who would commit a sexual assault or engage in sexual harassment, the responses echo the delusions: a stranger, scruffy, bad mannered, uneducated, distasteful, and the list continues in the negative. This is a false impression of the majority of offenders; they actually are routinely described as intelligent, handsome, outgoing, honorable, family-man, goal-orientated, charismatic, charming, and polite. This can add to the bewilderment of the victim. "Why would a nice guy rape me?" or "How can a nice guy do that?"

An additional myth about sexual assault is the view the aggressor is always someone who is unknown by the survivor; some stranger who jumps out of the bushes in the middle of the night. Contrary to that belief, in a survey conducted by the Department of Justice, 78% of the survivors knew their aggressor; whereas only 17% of the attackers were not known by the survivor. For MST survivors the rates of the survivor knowing the assailant is significantly higher because of many distinctive conditions involved. The higher increases of survivor knowing the aggressor is another unique aspect of MST.

When most people hear about sexual assault or sexual harassment they assign the victim to be a woman. Although a larger percentage of victims are women, men, who can also be the victims of either sexual harassment or sexual assault, account for a larger number of survivors of MST. The majority of soldiers are men, which accounts for there being a higher number, not a higher percentage, of male victims. For the remainder of this book, I will mostly be using a feminine pronoun to refer to the victims (survivors) of MST, only for consistency.

2
THE UNIQUENESS OF MST

Military Life

Military life is fundamentally different from civilian life in that –

    a. The extraordinary responsibility of the Armed Forces, the unique conditions of military service and the critical role of unit cohesion requires that the military community, which is subject to civilian control exist in a specialized society.

    b. The military society is characterized by its own laws, rules, customs, and traditions, including numerous restrictions on personal behavior, that would not be acceptable in civilian society (AR 600-20, 2008).

The military is not just a job; it is a way of life. "Air Force applicants must be morally and financially sound, not encumbered with dependency limitations for assignment availability or while on deployment" (AFRSI 36-2001, 2012). The military has its own language, laws, customs and traditions. At the core of the Armed Forces is protection of the United States, and this encompasses going to war. This culture can seem harsh at times, and be easily misunderstood.

Entering the military diminishes many personal and professional choices; choices civilians usually take for granted. These choices can be where an individual will train, sleep, eat, what to wear (including underwear), speak, how to reply to questions, go to bed, wake up, who will be in charge, and many, many more. All of the aforementioned will not be chosen by the individual, but directed by the military. Personal choices will also be curtailed. The military does not have to transfer these "privileges" back after initial training is completed. It can be said once a person joins the military, the military owns them. This concept is very difficult to comprehend for many who have not been in, or personally known a member of the military.

The standard of conduct for members of the Armed Forces regulate a member's life 24 hours each day beginning at the moment the member enters the military status and not ending

until the person is discharged or otherwise separated from the
Armed Forces (AR 600-20, 2008).

All choices have consequences, but when a member of the military makes a choice which is in opposition to the UCMJ, the consequences are extreme; prison time, court-martialed with dishonorable discharge, loss of pay, removal of rank, and this list continues. If a civilian worker decides they no longer want to work, they quit. In the military, for officers it is resigning their commission (if accepted and/or with serious career implications), for enlisted it can be dereliction of duty (or numerous other offences), and under the UCMJ, the result can be prison time. If a civilian does not want to live in their home any longer they can move. Depending on your status (with or without dependents), rank, the location, your job, and other conditions mandates your, optional or not optional, living quarters. You can request to be transferred to another unit, location, and so forth, but just as easily be denied (which could provoke intrusive questions). To be blunt, the military can control most of your life, which power of control is bestowed on a chain of command, and can trickle down to a person (supervisor) who usually is higher in rank than you. This power and authority over another's personal choices and their lives is easily abused.

All the Armed Forces have specific qualifications which must be met to be able to become a soldier – physical, mental and intellectual. Most do not know that truly unqualified applicants are allowed into the military with waivers. These waivers can be medical, mental, intellectual and even criminal (moral waivers). The history of the moral waiver goes back to the 1960's, but in the 2000's because of the continual need for more soldiers, more moral waivers were accepted, mostly from the Army. Just because a person wants to join the military, does not at all mean they should be allowed to. The military is not some desk job or selling cars. The potential possibly is placing a gun into a criminal's hand and giving them the means and ability to kill.

Quality applicants are those who have collectively high attributes of
educational, aptitude, physical, and moral standards. Recruitment of
these individuals is essential to the effective operation of the Air Force.
Meeting minimum enlistment qualifications does not guarantee

acceptance. Applicants are considered on a best-to-least qualified basis (Air Force Recruiting Service Instruction 36-2001, 1 August 2012).

So, why if the Armed Forces are seeking out the "quality" society has to offer, why are there moral waivers? Moral waivers are described as moral character wavier or moral conduct wavier; but in reality, they are all the same. A moral wavier is just what it states; it is a waiver of someone's morality so that they can join the Armed Services. These waivers have included, but are not at all limited to: misdemeanors; drug abuse; alcohol abuse; disorderly conduct; aggravated assaults; robbery; receiving stolen property; domestic assaults; suspected of murder and even making terrorist threats. Many studies have been conducted and the results were not a positive look for the Armed Forces as a whole. Too many soldiers with moral waivers went on to continue their criminal careers within the military, but were retained, promoted, even awarded medals. Inside the military these same criminal offenses, which if left to civilian authorities would accompany jail time, are allowed to continue with minor punishment (sometimes as little as a stern talking to) or no punishment at all. Allowing someone with certain aggressive criminal convictions, and/or substance abuses to use a moral wavier to enter the military is completely lowering the standards and putting the rest of the soldiers in danger. There are reasons for not allowing such dubious history to enter a career which requires the use of weapons, and the possibility of going to war.

The Army has the reputation of approving the most moral waivers. The Air Force and Coast Guard approve the fewest. The Navy and Marine Corps fall somewhere in between (Powers, usmilitary.about.com).

A small carrot for making sure our soldiers are the best, as well as helping eliminate many applicants whose behaviors are not conducive to the military, the National Defense Authorization Act for Fiscal Year 2013 was signed into law. Within the 681 pages falls: SEC. 523. Prohibition on waiver for commission or enlistment in the Armed Forces for individual convicted of a felony sexual offense. An individual may not be provided a waiver for commissioning or enlistment in the Armed Forces if the individual has been convicted under Federal or State law of a felony offense of any of the following: (1) Rape. (2) Sexual abuse. (3) Sexual assault. (4) Incest. (5) Any other sexual offense (National Defense Authorization Act, 2013).

There has been a vicious attack upon our American cultural values and traditions. It seems to come from all directions and the subculture of the military has not escaped. These attacks are purposeful and directed specifically at the family and the values of Christian beliefs. The attempt to rewrite history by deleting God out of pledges, oaths, schools, and the military, is an act of betrayal to all this country stands for. Whenever religion is mentioned as it relates within the confines of government, many cry out violently "separation of church and state." They mistakenly believe the quote is in the first amendment of the US Constitution, or any part of it. The statement was written by Thomas Jefferson, in a letter (not an official government document, as the Constitution is) to a church in 1802. Within the letter, Jefferson made it clear to the congregation that the government would not establish a national religion, as there had been in England. Our Founding Fathers were God-fearing men, and our country (as well as the Constitution) was intentionally founded on Biblical principles, not to the exclusion of religion but the inclusion of religious freedom, a very different concept. As this myth is continually allowed to be voiced, the actual Christian majority needs to come forward and stand for the truths we believe in. All that evil needs to thrive is for good men and women to do nothing.

The mission of the United States Air Force is to fly, fight and win…in air, space and cyberspace. To achieve that mission, the Air Force has a vision of Global Vigilance, Reach and Power. That vision orbits around three core competencies: developing Airmen, technology to war fighting and integrating operations (airforce.com).

The mission of the Navy is to maintain, train and equip combat-ready Naval forces capable of winning wars, deterring aggression and maintaining freedom of the seas (navy.com).

The Army's mission is to fight and win our Nation's wars by providing prompt, sustained land dominance across the full range of military operations and spectrum of conflict in support of combatant commanders (army.mil).

We are forward deployed to respond swiftly and aggressively in times of crisis. We are soldiers of the sea, providing forces and detachments to naval ships and shore operations... These capabilities make us "First to Fight" (marines.com).

The U.S. Coast Guard's mission is to protect the public, the environment, and U.S. economic interests – in the nation's ports and waterways, along the coast, on international waters, or in any maritime region as required to support national security (usg.mil).

Upon entering the military all individuals swear oaths to conduct themselves in a certain way, and to be subject to the UCMJ. As a recruit (officer or enlisted) furthers their training, other codes can be taken upon, drawing them closer, making them more cohesive to their specific military, to their specific career, and then their specific units. These smaller groups become more bonded with one another sharing a common mission. This connection is a powerful source of identity, need for loyalty and a deep sense of belonging; it becomes "family" and the profound emotional attachments involved are what they are looked to for: safety, sense of belonging, companionship, etc.

One of the most critical elements in combat capability is unit cohesion, that is, the bonds of trust among individual service members that make the combat effectiveness of a military unit greater than the sum of the combat effectiveness for the individual unit members (AR 600-20, 2008).

Another attack to American values and traditions is under the guise of "tolerance," and that "there really is not anything immoral, just a different point of view. "The presence in the Armed Forces of person's who demonstrate a propensity or intent to engage in homosexual acts would create an unacceptable risk to the high standards of morale, good order and discipline, and unit cohesion that are the essence of military capability." In the military, at many times, there is a lack of privacy for persons of the same sex; boot camp (basic training), ships, submarines, barracks, and on many deployments. These close quarters, which can be for long periods of time, make the military a unique working condition. Even if you believe the propensity of homosexual acts is not immoral, these chosen behavioral acts are not conducive to military life.

Military members are responsible to protect the United States from all foreign or domestic threats. This responsibility requires all military members to be able to handle weapons, and be in top physical and mental shape in case of need. All are trained for combat, whether or not they will see any has no bearing on their training.

The primary purpose of the armed Forces is to prepare for and to prevail in combat should the need arise (Title 10).

Combat training is taught in different levels of degree depending on the military and the job. It can be minimal; comprehending the positions of vehicles when attacked, knowing intricate details of the movement of a unit through enemy territory; to the extreme, hand-to-hand combat training. This type of combat training (hand-to-hand) is not a rough wrestling match. It is knowing how to respond when physically attacked or being the aggressor and attacking; all the while being able to protect yourself and inflicting as much injury (to death if necessary) on the other person as possible. This type of training is aggressive, vicious and physically demanding. Combat training is essential to the mission of the military, but also deadly when used to sexually assault another. At times the mental techniques involved with training lend to a more aggressive outlook on life, mottos from "peace is our profession, war is our capability" can get warped in some units internally changing the motto to "war is our profession, peace is our capability." It has not been too long ago when women were not allowed to be in combat units, or even combat career fields, and still today there are some fields shut. Whether or not a person agrees with this is not the purpose of this book, but because someone is in a non-combat field can mean they will not be trained to adequately protect themselves, even if they do experience combat. This gives many men, the larger part of are combat trained, the upper hand when assaulting women, especially when sufficient self-defense training has not been taught or required for all members.

Women in the military

Many women over the ages have been utilized in the militaries and especially during war-time; however, the first documented American woman soldier was Deborah Sampson. Ms. Sampson disguised herself as a man, enlisted in the Continental Army during the Revolutionary War, was wounded and eventually received an honorable discharge from General Washington.

In 1941, The Woman's Army Auxiliary Corps was created; however, it took until 1943, during World War II to become an official part of the US Army: Women's Army Auxiliary Corps. During that era, approximately 400,000 women participated in the war. After the war, most women returned to civilian life and in 1948 President Harry Truman allowed women to serve in the armed forces during peace time by signing the Women's Armed Services Integration Act, but limited the number of women serving to only 2% of the total military.

It is estimated during the Korean War, between 1950 and 1953, approximately 120,000 women served in the armed services (1,000 in theater). Women also served in the Vietnam War as support and medical personnel (7,500 in theater). During the 80's many women served in military operations such as Grenada (170 deployed) and Panama (770 deployed), but it was not until 1990/1991 during the Gulf War (Operation Desert Shield/Storm) that the role of women in the U.S. Armed Forces came to the attention of the world media. More than 41,000 women (in theater) served in almost every career field the forces had to offer, although were not officially "permitted" to participate in deliberate ground engagements, but as we all know, out in the field does not always correspond to policy.

The U.S. Census Bureau, 2013 American Community Survey, reported there were approximately **1,551,710,** women veterans (+/- 18,523, margin of error). In the *2013 Demographics Report, Profile of the Military Community* (militaryonesource.mil), the following numbers for women in active reserve and guard were as followed:

Active Duty

Air Force	61,803	19%
Navy	55,986	17%
Army	71,905	14%
Coast Guard	7,000	15%*
Marine Corps	14,201	7%
Total:	**210,895**	**15%**

Reserve & Guard

Army Reserve	45,382	23%
Air Force Reserve	18,486	26%
Navy Reserve	13,283	21%
Air National Guard	20,181	19%
Army National Guard	55,255	15%
Marine Corps Reserve	1,674	4%
Coast Guard Reserve	1,328	20%
Total:	**155,589**	**16.4%**

*(Coast Guard number approximate from uscg.mil, womencghistory.ppt).

3
BARRIERS TO REPORTING

Those reporting hostile work environments had approximately six-fold greater odds of rape (SARP, 2011).

In the US women are twice as likely to be physically assaulted at work than men, and more likely to die from workplace homicide than a job-related accident. Women in male-dominated occupations are at an escalated risk for harassment and physical assault. It is a commonplace occurrence for military women to come across workplace violence (2001, Sadler et al.).

Society has a history of utilizing feminine words as derogatory in nature. If a person is referred to as a "cry baby" they are being ridiculed to having infantile inabilities to control their behavior. This is understandable since infants do not possess the aptitude to fully control their emotions; however, a word like "ho," referring to a woman who is promiscuous (in the nicest terms), is feminine all the way. Then there is the word "sissy," which some say is derived from sister, but when another is called a "sissy" (other than by a four year old), they are not calling someone their sister; it is paralleled with weak, scrawny, and pathetic, not at all complimentary. The word "female" in the military culture has been associated with the same as saying weak, fragile and useless. I need not continue with this line of thought. We all know other unflattering names which are feminine. Women enter this military world with having the very nature of their sex being equivalent with everything that is not revered, but unconditionally detested.

When crimes happen, or when harassment occurs during civilian life, usually the investigating authority is a third party with no attachment to the incident. When the same occurs on a military installation with military members, or off-base with military members, the persons who are taking the complaint, taking a report, investigating the offense, trying the case, judging the issues, and/or handing down the punishment, customarily are all military, the same branch the members have joined, assigned to the same base, sometimes even within the same unit. Once traumatized, usually the woman questions whether it is better to keep quiet.

Some of the questions would be foreign to a civilian. Because military personnel fall under the UCMJ (Uniform Code of Military Justice), the law is different for them.

Questioning the victims, as if they had some responsibility involved in the incident, is not a new callous mind set. Often times, the victim is interrogated with questions like: "What were you wearing?," "Why were you walking alone?," "Why did you accept the drink?," and other such blaming queries. In the military another line of questioning can be used, and this deplorable technique is because the woman is often seen as making it up. Some of the questions lie around not just blaming the victim but catching the victim in some type of punishable behavior, referred to as collateral misconduct.

- 47% - indicated they or the offender had been drinking
- 2% - they or the offender had been using drugs before the incident (of the reported cases to military authority, WGRA, 2012).

Many reported sexual assaults involve circumstances where the victim may have engaged in some form of misconduct (i.e., underage drinking or other related alcohol offenses, adultery, fraternization or other violations of certain regulations or orders). Such behavior may be considered collateral misconduct, and may be viewed as a contributing factor to the sexual assault (preventsexualassault.armymil, 2015).

a. Collateral misconduct by the victim of a sexual assault is one of the most significant barriers to reporting assault because of the victim's fear of punishment. Some reported sexual assaults involve circumstances where the victim may have engaged in some form of misconduct (e.g., underage drinking or other related alcohol offenses, adultery, fraternization, or other violations of certain regulations or orders). Commanders shall have discretion to defer action on alleged collateral misconduct by the sexual assault victim (and shall not be penalized for such a deferral decision), until final disposition of the sexual assault case, taking into account the trauma to the victim and responding appropriately so as to encourage reporting of sexual assault and continued victim cooperation, while also bearing in mind any potential speedy trail and statute of limitations concerns.

Under the UCMJ, the most important decisions about the investigation and prosecution, in most instances, fall to the commander. If the commander has already displayed his/her allowance of sexual harassment under their command or leniency toward perpetrators (of both sexual harassment and/or sexual assault), the fear of telling increases dramatically. Historically the military has a habit of wanting to deal with problems within its own chain of command, and in the past regulations gave pretty much total control to the commanders.

Commanders were usually given the discretion to resolve complaints internally and had a tremendous influence on the disposition of cases, whether it is officially documented/reported, forwarded for criminal investigation, or dropped with no further action. This commander was not necessarily a Base Commander who is assigned over other squadron/platoon commanders, but could have been several different levels in the chain of command; squadron/platoon commander, a Wing Commander, and a Base Commander, to name a few.

Along the chain of command are superiors who can influence a victim to be: talked out of reporting for fear of retaliation; coerced into believing it was just a misunderstanding; told they would not be believed; made to feel as though it was the victim's fault; and other such deceptive persuasions to keep their command or the perpetrator from repercussions. Because of the way rank is acquired in the military, some members have no problems silencing potential rank or career damaging dilemmas. There may never be true statistics of how many have been sexually assaulted or sexually harassed because many incidents never reached beyond the commander's office.

Reviewing decades of media worthy cases, each response, by the branch of military under the spot-light, has suspiciously been condensed to the incidents being "abnormal," "unusual," "uncharacteristic," "astonishing," and blame had been placed on a few "deviant members." Taking just the military's own officially reported cases into account, it is clear the ones that hit the media were not "unusual" at all. A staggering majority of them had been leaked to an outside agency, through family members, friends, even the victims themselves.

The irritation many commands broadcast towards an outsider (to question about the allegations) coming into their territory and just asking questions can resonate as the survivor being labeled a trouble maker, causing unnecessary waves, and result in the survivor becoming an outcast within her own unit. Fear of being cast in the same image as the branded trouble maker leads to many of her friends and peers distancing themselves, causing a sense of additional isolation and loneliness for the survivor.

- 33% - most dissatisfied with commanders handling the report (of the members who made a report to military authority)
- 66% - felt uncomfortable making a report
- 50% - did not think anything would be done (WGRA, 2012).

I thought they were my friends that's until the investigation was out, then it was like I had the plague. No one wanted to be by someone they knew who had been targeted. – Army Veteran

MST often occurs in a setting where the survivor lives and works. Military members are usually stationed away from their hometowns, away from family and friends, who could be support systems, but are distantly unavailable. When deployed, the support system, if any, is drastically limited. The survivor of MST can be relying on her assailant for back up, sometimes causing the choice of telling to literally be a life or death decision.

- 23% - afraid of being assaulted by the offender (reasons why victim did not make a report)
- 67% - reports indicated at a military installation
- 41% - of the reports were during work/duty hours (where/when assaults happened, WGRA, 2012)

The worldwide deployment of United States military forces, the international responsibilities of the United States, and the potential for involvement of the Armed Forces in actual combat routinely make it necessary for members of the Armed Forces involuntarily to accept living conditions and working conditions that are often Spartan, primitive, and characterized by forced intimacy with little or no privacy (AR 600-20, 2008).

Perpetrators are often the survivor's peers, in the chain of command, and/or her own supervisor, which usually leads to disruptions of, if not the end of, her military career goals. This adds to the probability she will have to continue to work with or live near the perpetrator. Along with disruption of goals, the perpetrator is usually in a decision making position for performance evaluations, promotions, even designating where she will work. At times, this places the decision upon the survivor to either be forced to leave the military for protection (depleting all her military career goals and the advantages of staying in the military), or have frequent contact with the perpetrator, igniting horrendous stress and the likely risk for further victimization.

The assailants were:

- 57% - military coworkers
- 25% - someone in their chain of command
- 38% - higher rank/grade not in their chain of command (WGRA, 2012).

Many times the victim is told "if it is too much, you just need to leave;" "get away from the perpetrator;" "change jobs;" and other such advice from nonmilitary understanding individuals. If the abuser is your coworker or in your chain of command (statistics show it usually is), there is nowhere you can legally escape to. Running means AWOL, and that means court-martial and possible prison time. There are no sick days attached to the papers that were signed when entering the military. Some units require you to be in the hospital, or be put on quarters from a doctor to be excused from duty. Requesting leave is just that, a request, which usually first must be approved by the supervisor (possibly the assailant), and then can be dependent on the duty of the person, mission of their position, and/or location of the installation. Even if leave is available, other check lists must also be approved; therefore, just leaving is not such a practical option.

- 12% - was in a location where the member could not contact authority (WGRA, 2012).

In the fiscal year 2013, there were 301 reports of sexual assault in "Combat areas of Interest," which is a 26% increase in overall reporting from fiscal 2012. There was a 17% increase of unrestricted reports, 247, but a 107% increase from the 28 initial restricted reports in FY2012 to the initial 58 in FY2013. The amounts and locations of the unrestricted reports:

- 142 – Afghanistan (57%)
- 23 – Iraq (11%)
- 21 – Kuwait
- 16 – Qatar
- 15 – Bahrain
- 11 – United Arab Emirates
- 5 – Jordan
- 4 – Djibouti
- 3 – Oman
- 3 – Egypt
- 3 – Kyrgyzstan
- 1 – Saudi Arabia

Amounts and locations of the initial 58 restricted reports:

- 26 – Afghanistan
- 11 – Iraq
- 7 – Kuwait
- 6 – Qatar
- 2 – Bahrain
- 2 – Kyrgyzstan
- 2 – United Arab Emirates
- 1 – Egypt
- 1 – Saudi Arabia (FY2013, DoD Annual Report).

In a study, (Finn, 1995) derived from college/university campuses across the US, findings displayed that a significant number of women abandoned their education (many left in midterm not even officially withdrawing), and left the area for their parents'/friends' residence back in their hometowns'. Several victims returned to a place where they felt safe: this being a parent's home, a long-time friend's home, or just back an area that had lived before.

"Acquaintance rape victims suffer the same psychological harms as stranger-rape victims: shock, humiliation, anxiety, depression, substance abuse, suicidal thoughts, loss of self-esteem, social isolation, anger, distrust of others, fear of AIDS, guilt, and sexual dysfunction. College acquaintance rape victims face additional consequences. Many drop out of school because, if they stay, they might regularly face their attacker in class, in their dorm, in the dining hall, or at campus functions and events" (Sampson, 2002).

Military members normally do not have the option to "drop out," and the area in which the abuse occurred usually has to be revisited on a daily basis (dorm room, work place). Sometimes it is not only the area, but the assailant is regularly seen, and not by want of the victim. Once a trauma occurs, the military has had the "suck-it-up" mentality, and expects your performance to be at least equal to, usually increasing, after the attack.

- 37% - waited until they felt safe from the offender (why the report was made after 24 hours, WGRA, 2012).

Retaliation is also another fear, which numerous military victims have described as being incessant, vicious, and from all parts of the unit. The commander of a unit usually sets the atmosphere for the troops under it. If his/her response in the past towards victims has been indifferent or reproachful concerning the allegations, this often leads to allowance of continual harassment and abuse, causing many victims to deem it better to keep quiet than to face additional torment. There are too many accounts where victims endured:

- unfounded negative paperwork in their files;
- threatened with punitive action;
- harassed;
- ostracized by their peers;
- ordered to counseling;
- received bad postings;
- put on postings which were high risk for injury or death;
- declared not be able to perform their jobs anymore and be discharged;
- assigned another (lower) position;
- assigned to another base/post, or unit, against their wishes;
- diagnosed with Borderline Personality Disorder and discharged (or another mental condition);

- ordered to be placed on duty in a war zone without their weapon.
- restricted to the base;
- ordered to work with their abuser;
- given unfounded paperwork (Letters of Counseling, Letters of Reprimand);
- used the unfounded paperwork to establish a pattern and were discharged;
- denied leave;
- and ordered to work when they were not scheduled.

And, what can they do if this happens? Report it? Look where that route took them in the first place.
- 17% - threatened to ruin the victims reputation if they did not consent
- 31% - experienced social retaliation (of the reports made to military authority, WGRA, 2012).

- 47% - afraid of retaliation/reprisal from person who did it or their friends
- 47% - thought they would be labeled a troublemaker
- 35% - thought performance evaluation would change
- 23% - feared others would be punished
- 15% - thought lose security clearance (why the incident was not reported, WGRA, 2012).

Some interesting information which was accessed from the 2001, Sadler et al study was that a majority of women, after they had been sexually assaulted, did not seek emotional counseling or medical help. The physical assault negatively affected their feelings about self-esteem, emotional health and their physical condition. When unwelcome sexual advances, pressures for dates, and remarks occurred in/around the victim's sleeping quarters, there was a seven-fold increase of physical assault. This increased risk tripled when ranking officers allowed sexually demeaning comments and/or behaviors in their units, or the officers made the remarks themselves. There were consistent rates of physical assaults across all eras of all the services.

In the first Survivor Experience Survey (2014) from the Defense Research, Surveys, and Statistics Center (RRS), out of 782 tickets generated, 151 surveys from sexual assault survivors were counted as completed. The data, which limitations caused by selected strategies to reach out to the sexual assault survivors cannot be generalized to all military sexual survivors, but is still significant. Tickets were generated to allow the survivors to take the survey anonymously and in privacy. The sampling criteria, which was collected from June 4, 2014 to September 22, 2014, consisted of: uniformed members; 18 years and up; who made restricted/unrestricted report for any form of sexual assault; and made the report at least 30 days prior to taking the survey, but after October 1, 2013. In the report, of the 80% who made an unrestricted report, a staggering 59% of respondents, believed they experienced social retaliation to some extent (27% to a *large extent*, 12% to a *moderate extent*, and 20% to a *small extent*) since they reported their sexual assault. A little less than that, 40%, disclosed they had experienced professional retaliation (20% to a *large extent*, 10% to a *moderate extent*, and 9% to a *small extent*).

Unit cohesiveness can create an environment where survivors are strongly influenced to keep quiet about their experiences, have their reports ignored, or be dealt with within the unit itself. This camaraderie is needed for the intense possibility of relying on one another to have your back. Although this needed bond can keep units together in times of serious conflict, it can also be used to silence another member about the incident. When one of the members of the unit is accusing another member, lines are drawn, friends are aligned, and mouths tighten up. Unfortunately because an allegation of sexual assault or sexual harassment can be a stain on the unit, and on the military, most ally themselves with the perpetrator.

When someone is assaulted or harassed, and it is done by their brother/sister-in-arms, further adding to the trauma, MST survivors suffer extreme familial betrayal similar to incest survivors, but without sympathetic statements such as "You were too young to understand" or "He was an adult and twice the size of you." Additionally, MST survivors endure the intense mental contradiction that one of their duties in being a soldier is protecting the United States, yet feel as though they could not even protect themselves.

A significant amount of victims do not disclose the abuse because of the stigma associated with mental illness, which their symptoms indicate. The stigma toward mental health has an intensely negative effect on an individual's social intermingling, treatment seeking conduct, and self-esteem. Within the military community self-reliance and inner strength are greatly relished. Mental illness can be judged as a flaw and motive for humiliation, causing people to disregard or deny their illness and/or avoid seeking care once diagnosed.

In several studies of active duty members, before and after deployment, toward accessing mental health, there were several common negative themes: their feelings and views about the stigma; damage to a person's career; and what seeking care would mean for continuation in the military. As a result only a small number of those in need of services actually sought them.

Another major question, "Who's going to know if I tell?" The added trauma of just reporting sexual assault or sexual harassment is enough without the additional trauma of everybody knowing. Prior to the recent implementation limiting commanders to disclose details of the incident, the commander could ask whomever he wanted and disclose whatever he wanted. Still now the list of individuals who will be contacted because of the accusations is not limited to the victim, witnesses, and the investigating authority. The list is actually too large to effectively write out, but to understand the possibilities: her immediate supervisor, First Sergeant, unit commander, Platoon Commander, Wing Commander, Base Commander, then her co-workers, her roommate(s), the accused's supervisor, and on and on. Even when an investigation is reported under the new restricted form, there are so many ways details leaks out.

In the civilian world, when these assaults of maltreatment occur the list of individuals which will have access to and know about the investigation is limited. It may be only a few people if the case does not get prosecuted. Numerous military women find out exactly how many people "became involved" in the investigation once it is out. The list started with the person she told, then on to the commander, then the commander could ask any person he/she deemed "necessary" to determine his/her next step at the commander's discretion, not the victim's. There are too many stories from survivors describing how "everybody" knew, whether that person really needed to know (or be asked questions) or not.

- 51% - did not think it would be kept confidential
- 32% - thought about getting out of the service (reported cases, WGRA, 2012).

Believability is an understandable concern many woman face when telling. This is further compounded in the military, when it is not just your word against his, but your rank against his. Rank is power. It is not just the issue of the single woman against the family man. It is the E-1, considered a nothing in terms of rank, without any weighted time in the military, alone, without family and long-time friends, against the E-5 (or pick another higher rank it just adds to the rank power), who is at least on his second term, one of the good ole boys, with family, military friends, and nothing in his file to say otherwise (because the allegations of the last four times were dropped by his previous commander and there are NO records kept of that). Who do you think they will side with? It will not be given a second thought. Without looking into any part of the facts, whether there is physical evidence, witnesses or anything else, the guy will be believed.

- 43% - did not think they would be believed
- 43% - heard about negative experiences other victims went through who reported
- 50% - did not think anything would be done
- 23% - afraid of being assaulted again by the offender (why the victim did not report, WGRA, 2012).

I told my Shirt, he told the Commander and then it was like everyone knew. My supervisor, my roommate, practically everyone who worked around me and it did not stop there. When someone would say that I had sex with some guy, they asked him! Some of the guys they asked I had never even met, it was all rumors. What did it have to do with (the rape)? – Air Force Reserve Veteran.

After all other obstacles have been hurtled, and the allegations are validated, the degrees of punishments handed down would astonish an intelligent individual. Even if an allegation is substantiated the wide-ranging diversities of punishments can range from: a verbal reprimand (a stern talking to); a letter in the perpetrator's unit file (which does not leave with the perpetrator once he has departed that unit); a fine (usually minimal); loss of rank (usually just one stripe); confined to base (grounded); a letter of counseling; a letter of reprimand; an Article 15; and/or court-martial. Some of the most recognizable cases, which allegations vary from forcible sodomy, rape, and threatening death to the raped victim if they told anyone, were disciplined with: removal of a command, a General discharge from the military and three months in jail with the loss of rank (one pay grade), respectively. With such incompatible disciplinary actions dispensed for these horrendous crimes, why would a woman believe she could receive justice? When the time does not fit the crime, why would it not continue to be so pervasive? Most survivors are given camouflaged answers to their cases. These answers mainly state that the allegations have been proven or unproven, that the alleged perpetrator had disciplinary action taken against him, or the commander took appropriate action - purposefully vague. Unlike civilian courts, when a military member is reprimanded, the victim does not have the right to know the punishment. Unless the case went to court-martial or information leaked as to what the "sentence" given was, the victim is usually left out in the dark.

- 26% - victim received combination of professional/social administration action or punishments
- 2% - victim received administrative action only (of the members who reported to military authority
- Noted there was no category for punishment only (WGRA, 2012).

In FY2013 Commanders processed 56 subjects in sexual assault investigation for administrative discharge. Only one member was retained after facing and administrative discharge board. The following discharges were conferred: Honorable Discharge – 1, General Discharge – 30, Under Other Than Honorable Conditions – 10, Uncharacterized – 7, and Pending Characterization – 7.

Even under the Freedom of Information Act, receiving documents about the incidents can look like a Top Secret report, with most of the important information (names, dates, places) blackened out. The confidentiality clause respected the rights of the assailant, but the victims' were tossed out the window. Many women never reported the continuation of abuse they endured because of fear, embarrassment, and retaliation once the statements were made.

- 21% - stated if they could do it again they would not report the same way (reported unrestricted, WGRA, 2012).

He raped me. I sat there as the commander said it was better we kept this within. He got a letter in his file, and then a few months later he was still promoted. He raped me and he was promoted, how do you think I felt? – Air Force Veteran, Iraq

Sexual Assault Prevention and Response

The Armed Forces might reply to the above particulars by relating that this could have happened in the past (prior to 2006). There is now a Sexual Assault Prevention and Response Office which on its website states "the single point of accountability for Department of Defense (DoD) sexual assault policy." With these new guidelines, new regulations and "zero tolerance" policies, it would seem the DoD has taken the appropriate steps to curtail this abuse, but do not be deceived. The pervasiveness of sexual assault and sexual harassment is not new to any branch of service. There have been surveys, investigations, and studies; yet none (of the military services) has come forward and stated there was or is a serious problem. You do not have to respond to a problem if you do not admit that it is a problem.

These guidelines, regulations and reporting agencies are still within the system of the military, subject to many of the same numerous inconsistencies of the past. The individuals who are the "new advocates" for the victims are usually military members, and subject to a chain of command. A shocking piece of information learned by browsing the regulations (2005) was the previous highly inferior qualifications of the Victim Advocate and SARC Coordinator. From the beginning it seemed the military really did not want a successful program. The tossing together of minimal qualifications of individuals whose secondary job was one of an "advocate" seemed to be the norm. The policy allowed a soldier to become a VA even as a perpetrator with a history of domestic violence, as long as the last incident happened over five (5) years ago.

The UVAS will be selected in accordance with the following requirements: Soldier will not have a recent history (within the past five years) of domestic violence, significant indebtedness, excess use of alcohol, or any use of illegal drugs. Must not have been punished under the provisions of the UCMJ during the 5 years preceding the nomination (www.sexualassault.army.mil).

More appropriate qualifications, including training and education, have trickled into the regulations over the years; however, the position of Victim Advocate is still secondary to the member's actual job. No VA or SARC should have ANY history as a perpetrator of domestic violence, sexual harassment, sexual assault, indecent exposure, or any other crime relating to aggression/violence of a sexual nature. Allowing such substandard qualifications demonstrate exactly how the DoD really viewed sexual assault/harassment.

What was I to do? (The commander) did it, and he (SARC) reported to him. – Army, Active Duty

Later I found out they (the perpetrator and Victim Advocate) were buddies, and nobody thought this was a problem. – Navy, Active Duty

The policies, procedures, and requirements of training (of Sexual Assault Response Coordinator, Victim Advocate, and Health Care Personnel in regard to sexual assaults) now falls to the Sexual Assault Prevention and Response Office, along with accumulating the statistics to show trends and formulate new policies. Looking over some of the programs, there is a pattern of concern.

When a sexual assault occurs the victim decides which route, she would like to take -- restricted or unrestricted. The first concern is that the victim has just been assaulted and must make the formidable decision about who will know; if the assault will be investigated; protection from the assailant; and more is being asked of her. Her mental and emotional state can be compromised because of the trauma. Even complete explanation of the decision does not guarantee the victim has understood, or even consciously heard the explanation.

The restricted method...
Allows a sexual assault victim to confidentially disclose the details of his or her assault to specified individuals and receive medical treatment and counseling, without triggering the official investigative process. Service members who are sexually assaulted and desire restricted reporting under this policy may only report the assault to the SARC (Sexual Assault Response Coordinator), VA (SAPR Victim Advocate), or a HCP (Health care Provider or Personnel).

Healthcare personnel will initiate the appropriate care and treatment, and report the sexual assault to the SARC in lieu of reporting the assault to law enforcement or the command.

Within 24 hours of Service...the SARC will inform the Senior Commander that an assault has occurred and provide the Commander with non-identifying personal information/details related to the sexual assault allegation. This information can include: rank; gender; age; race; service; date; time; and/or location. Within smaller units with only two of the above detailed information a victim's identity could be known.

The Senior Commander may notify the Criminal Investigators. However, no criminal investigation will be initiated unless originated from another source.

Limitations:
- Your assailant cannot be held accountable and may be capable of assaulting other victims.
- You cannot receive a military protective order.
- You will continue to have contact with your assailant, if he/she is in your organization or billeted with you.

- Evidence from the crime scene where the assault occurred will be lost, and the official investigation, should you switch to an Unrestricted Report, will likely encounter significant obstacles.
- You will not be able to discuss the assault with anyone, to include your friends, without imposing an obligation on them to report the crime. The only exceptions would be chaplains, designated healthcare personnel, your assigned SAPR VA, SARC, and Special Victims Counsel (www.sapr.mil, 2015).

If the Senior Commander does notify criminal investigations, by nature of their wanting to know all that goes on under their command, it is not likely there will not an inquiry, be it covert. Plus what investigator does not like to solve a mystery - the assault? The disclaimer that would enable the investigators to commence an investigation, even though the case was restricted, is if another source originates the information about the assault. Keeping any type of information quiet in a unit is challenging, especially the hint someone in the unit has made sexual assault/harassment allegations. This is one reason many victims decide to not tell anyone in the first place.

An apprehension about this reporting style is that you are unable to discuss the assault, making it a secret. This binds the victim to silence about what occurred. This realization adds additional strain onto the victim because if she discloses the assault, or somehow it is blurted out, she has now placed the listener into a pickle.

Another concern, and most distressing limitation, of reporting "restricted" is if rumors about the assault resulted in command becoming aware of misconduct, the victim can be charged with any number of offenses under the UCMJ. Under restricted reporting you are ineligible to invoke the collateral misconduct provision of the Department's sexual assault policy in the event that your command learns that you had been engaged in some form of misconduct at the time you were assaulted.

"e. Commanders shall have the authority to determine, in a timely manner, how to best manage the disposition of alleged misconduct, to include making the decision to defer disciplinary actions regarding a victim's alleged collateral misconduct until after the final disposition of the sexual assault case, where appropriate. For those sexual assault cases for which the victim's alleged collateral misconduct is deferred, Military Service reporting and processing requirements should take such deferrals into consideration and allow for the time deferred to be subtracted, when evaluating whether a commander took too long to resolve the collateral misconduct" (DoDI 6495.02, March 28, 2013).

It would appear that unrestricted would be the best way to proceed, but the same problematic results ensue. The unrestricted option "is recommended for victims of sexual assault who desire an official investigation and command notification in addition to healthcare, victim advocacy and legal services" (sapr.mil, 2015). If you select to use unrestricted reporting you are instructed to "use current reporting channels, e.g.:

- Law Enforcement/MCIO (will initiate an investigation and start a "report of investigation")
- Commander (who will then immediately contact the MCIO to start a "report of investigation")
- Sexual Assault Response Coordinator (SARC) (who will fill out a report with the "DD Form 2910" where the victim elects to reporting option)
- SAPR Victim Advocate (SAPR VA) (who will fill out a report with the "DD Form 2910")
- Health care personnel (who will then immediately contact the SARC to fill out the "DD Form 2910")

Upon notification of a reported sexual assault, the SARC will immediately assign a SAPR VA. At the victim's discretion or request, the healthcare personnel shall conduct a sexual assault forensic examination (SAFE), which may include the collection of evidence" (sapr.mil, 2015).

The considerations, listed by SAPR, when selecting an unrestricted report:

- Victims feel a sense of closure or healing which can aid recovery.

- Ability for Military to hold the offender appropriately accountable.
- Ensure the safety of the victim and others, who may be victimized by the same suspect.
- Ability to request a Military Protective Order.
- Ability to request an Expedited Transfer to move to a different base (sarp.mil, 2015).

In an Executive Summary of the DoD, for the calendar year 2004, out of 1,700 reported sexual assaults there were only 113 courts-martial. There were 340 offenders still being processed for final action at the end of that year, but 278 offenders were placed into the "un-identified offender/punitive action not possible," and 351 offenders in the "unsubstantiated, unfounded, insufficient evidence" category. Because most assault survivors know their attackers, it is highly unlikely the "un-identified offender, punitive action not possible" category was weighted on the un-identified side. The designation not only includes an un-identified offender, but adds that punitive action was not possible without any more details, to suggest the action was only not possible because the offender was not known.

In the DoD *Annual Report on Sexual Assault in the Military, Fiscal Year 2013*, the total number of unrestricted reports was 3,768, of that 3,195 were the number of reports involving service members as victims. The MCIOs initiated 3,642 sexual assault investigations with the length of these depending on: the offense alleged; the location and availability of the victim, subject, and witness; the amount and type of physical evidence gathered during the investigation; and the length of time required for crime laboratory analysis of evidence. So, the investigations and their outcomes can span multiple reporting periods. It would be beneficial for the investigation cases to have their own user-friendly reports to their final disposition without limiting them to reporting periods. It is mentioned that the outcomes of the investigations (1,460), which were opened but not completed in FY2013, will be documented in future reports.

In FY2013, there were 2,149 Service member subjects, who were under the legal authority of the Department, investigated for sexual assault in fiscal year 2013. Of the 2,149 subjects, commanders were unable to take action against 522 because:

- Victims declined to participate in justice action – 189 subjects
- Insufficient evidence of any offense to prosecute – 34 subjects
- Statute of limitations expired – 9 subjects.

For 58 of the subjects the allegations were stated to be unfounded by Command/Legal Review. The command has sufficient evidence and legal authority to support some form of disciplinary action for 1,569 military subjects. For 382 subjects the command stated the evidence only supported an action on a non-sexual assault offense (e.g., adultery, making a false statement, underage drinking, or other crimes under the UCMJ). Of them (382):

- Court-martial charge was preferred (initiated) – 34 subjects
- Nonjudicial punishment (Article 15, UCMJ) – 215 subjects
- Administrative discharge – 43 subjects
- Other adverse administrative action – 90 subjects.

There were 1,187 subjects for which sexual assault offense action was taken:

- Court-martial charge preferred (initiated) – 838 subjects (71%)
- Nonjuducual punishment (Article 15, UCMJ) – 210 subjects (18%)
- Administrative discharge – 56 subjects
- Other adverse administrative action – 83 subjects.

At the end of the fiscal year 2013, there were 3,858 subjects receiving or waiting for a disposition for the allegations against them; however, the above is a stark contrast from fiscal year 2004.

Even with all the new laws are regulations, the number of women veterans reported to have been sexually assaulted, or reported to have dealt with sexual harassment has not decreased significantly. It is hard to account for all the reports of sexual trauma for several reasons. The militaries do not have one universal system for reporting all official and non-official reports of sexual assault and sexual harassment, it has not been mandatory for a superior to report what has been disclosed to him, or a commander to report what has been kept in-house, even if the allegations were founded and there was action taken against the assailant. The various ways an "investigation" could have gone, whether it was passed onto the Military Police (in the Air Force, Security Forces, previously called Security Police), or kept in the unit or under the same command, accounts for many reports which were never documented. Many survivors still find going outside their commands the only way they feel they will be listened to, where a report will be documented and hopefully some action taken against the accused. This has been a serious criticism of the system for decades. Numbers vary greatly from one study to the next, each annotating the deficiencies, but none of the militaries to date have drastically changed to account for the majority of unwanted sexual contact and harassment, as a whole.

In recent years, a hearing on C-Span about MST to US House Committee Armed Services, each of the military's own representatives tried claiming their military was so different from the others that a universal reporting and/or universal way these allegations are handled is impossible. Even with SAPR, each of the militaries still have their own policy, procedures, and regulations.

4
RESPONSES

I found myself shaking, not being able to breath; I didn't know what was going on. I knew I hadn't seen him, it looked like him, but it wasn't, it couldn't be. Why am I acting like this? What's wrong with me? – Navy, Active Duty.

Veterans and active duty members report a wide range of sexually victimizing experiences, which span from inappropriate sexual jokes, requests for sexual favors, pressure to have sex, to forcible rape. The range of emotional reactions is just as wide. There is no one way a survivor will respond, just as there is no one way a survivor should respond; the time to respond is just as variant. Each survivor will respond and react to their own unique experience(s), in their own particular time, in their own individual way. These reactions may last for several hours, days, weeks, months, and even years; be mild, moderate or severe.

Some common emotional, physical and psychological reactions are: (Note - If you have *any* of the reactions in bold, please seek immediate help)

- Aggression
- Anger
- **Anxiety (panic attack)**
- Avoidance (of people, places or things)
- **Begin or increased use/abuse of alcohol or drugs (illegal, prescription, over-the-counter, cigarettes, caffeine, coffee, sugar)**
- Denial
- **Depression**
- Detachment
- Difficulty concentrating
- Difficulty trusting
- Disbelief
- **Disoriented or out of touch with reality**
- Changes in appetite
- Embarrassment
- Fear
- **Feeling out of control**
- Feelings of helplessness

- **Flashbacks**
- Guilt
- Headaches
- **Homicidal thoughts with or without a plan**
- Hypervigilance
- Irritability
- Isolation
- Loss of intimacy
- **Loss of periods of time**
- Need to control
- Nightmares
- **Not being able to stop thinking about the incident**
- Numbness
- Panic
- Risky behaviors
- Self-blame
- Shame
- Shock
- Sleeplessness
- Spiritual crisis
- Stomach aches
- **Suicidal Ideation with or without a plan**
- **Thoughts of self-harm**
- Unable to experience joy or love

I sleep with my bed away from the windows in case someone comes in. – Army Veteran.

Understand that you are not going nuts, losing your mind, or going off the deep end. You have experienced a sexual trauma. Your reactions are normal and there is no shame in them. Your feelings and emotions from the experience(s) are neither good nor bad; they just are. Feelings and emotions are neutral. The perception we assign them places them into categories.

Anger

Anger is said to help people during life's difficulties, supplying them with increased energy to persevere in the face of obstacles. As a core element of the survival response in humans, it is usually a fundamental feature of a survivor's reaction. Anger is a normal initial response to trauma, feelings of being victimized, being out of control, and unfair events. In life, when threatening situations happen, anger can trigger brain activity, chemical releases, and amplify physical energy, resulting in the fight, flight, or freeze reaction to survive.

Although a normal response to trauma, anger, which is uncontrolled or inappropriate to the current circumstances, can cause serious problems for the survivor. It can result in difficulties at work, with family members, and interfere with personal intimate relationships as well as the self-image of the victims. Because anger can keep others at a distance, you can be unconsciously using it in an attempt to stay safe. The logic behind your use is because someone hurt you; if you do not allow anyone near you, you cannot be hurt again. This anger can resonate toward many righteous targets: the perpetrator, the system, the laws or lack of. Sometimes this anger points inward at the survivor causing the common outcome to be self-blame. You would never blame another for what happened to them, but looking at your own situation, thoughts of self-blame come into and linger in your mind; you think it somehow was different in your case. There are several reasons that these judgments happen. Many have to do with our culture of interlocking sex with violence.

The Media has portrayed acts of violence and intimacy occurring simultaneously so often that it is viewed as a normal occasion. How many times has the media displayed the following: a man and woman in a heated argument, the woman slaps the man, the man then returns the slap, and seconds later they cannot rip their clothes off fast enough? The scene continues as the man slams the woman against the wall in some presumed heated and excited state, as she digs her nails into his back, they forcibly kiss. The viewed outcome is the two of them exhausted, naked, on the bed, and allegedly satisfied. With these types of distorted intimate scenes how can the true repulsive nature of sexual assaults be comprehended by the masses? Unfortunately, too many times the media suggests that a woman saying no just means that you are not aggressively persuasive enough for it to change into a yes. The point is clear, no means "NO!" When anyone says the word no, whether it be screamed out, muffled under a hand, sternly conveyed, softly pleaded, or even mouthed without words...IT IS NO!!!

This "no" also includes other verbal forms: stop, don't, end it, cut it out, quit, leave, get out, and others. Verbal is not the only method that "no" comes in. Non-verbal forms can be: being pushed away; removing a hand; twisting; backing up; shaking of a head; cringing; squirming; and shrinking. These are not exclusive, and just because a woman has not displayed the above does in no terms mean the course of action is desired. A woman can be incapable of verbally or physically rejecting the advances. Being under the influence of any type of substance, which diminishes your mental capacities, like drugs (illegal, prescription and/or over the counter) and/or alcohol, can impair the ability to verbally or physically express objections, but that does not mean you gave your consent. You did not. It was assault.

I just get angry, don't know why, just angry. – Marine Corps, Active Duty.

I snapped at her (daughter) for no reason. I was just frustrated. – Navy Veteran.

It's shameful. . . the rage. . . don't have any reason for it. – Veteran, WASP.

Remembering the argument, it was stupid, but I couldn't control the feeling, total anger. – Air Force Veteran.

Guilt

Along with self-blame, survivors tend to reflect back on the experience wondering, "What if I had done this differently?" You can fixate on what you did, what you judged to be the reasons for the assault, and/or what you could have done that would have changed the outcome. These thoughts can also be considered another form of self-blame. Although you might say that it was the perpetrator who committed the offense, you could believe you had some responsibility in what occurred. It is not your behavior which defines sexual assault/harassment. It is the actions of the offender. The "what if" never seems to be directed to anything worse than what actually happened. You can fixate on why you did not fight, and fantasize that if you had fought the outcome would have been more positive. What about if you had fought and instead the outcome was worse? "What ifs" seem to always be positive.

fantasizing about a better outcome, but it could have been a worse outcome too. There is no reason to continue to create more blame. It was NOT your fault in ANY way.

Unfortunately, many argue the assumed reasons for the assault were the victim's. We make thousands of choices every day, some are considered good, others can be neutral or bad. Sometimes the only reason a choice is placed into the bad column is because of the outcome. I decided one day to go and check my mail, which happens to be at the end of a long red clay dirt road. The sky did not look too bleak, so I headed out without my umbrella. I was just about to open the mail box, and as most will tell you, Texas weather happened, it dumped on me. I ran back through the newly soaked mud ruining the pants I was wearing. My decision to leave without an umbrella only became a "bad" choice because of the rain. Had I gone to the mail box and back before the downpour, I would not have ruined my pants, and it would have just been another walk to the mailbox. This illustrates how a seemingly neutral choice, not taking the umbrella, led to what I considered to be a bad choice. Other choices, such as drinking and getting into a car, can be seen as bad to some from the beginning, without the conclusion of an assault. We are allowed to make even bad choices, but that does not mean anyone has a right to assault us. Making yourself vulnerable is also not a "green light" to being assaulted. There is only one choice that makes any difference, and that one choice was the perpetrator choosing to assault you. Be careful with "what if" thoughts, as they usually lead to pointing the finger in the mirror, and that is not where the problem or accountability lies. All blame lies solely on the assailant. There is no shame or guilt involved with being a victim. Those feelings, however unlikely, should fall entirely on the perpetrator.

The emotion of guilt is a common response to a traumatic experience and associated with the perceived or real perception of **wrongdoing**. This guilt is connected to a self-condemnation and responsibility a person feels for something they did, did not do or thought they should have done. There is a sense of wishful thinking, that somehow had I done this or not done that; the outcome would turn to something more positive. The real fact of the matter is nobody knows what the outcome would have been and the only thought that it would have been better is limited and unrealistic. Many blame themselves for the incident ever happening, even though they had no control over the situation. Countless individuals overestimate their precognitive knowledge of the events, referred to as hindsight bias. These were not normal situations; the person did not have all the time in the world to make a decision, all the facts and outcomes were not totally known, and assessing responsibility of these experiences based on these false assumptions can lead to a person getting stuck in their guilt.

A person can feel as though they must have done something really wrong to feel this awful, or that they would be a monster if they did not feel guilty. Feelings are not truth, just because a person feels bad does not make them so, and it also does not mean the omission or commission of some act they did was bad either.

Another misconception about a person's guilt is assessing complete responsibility for the entire traumatic event. As if that person was completely in control of not only their own actions but also that they could control other's actions, even nature itself. In many different articles referring to this guilt, a survivor can take complete irrational and inaccurate responsibility for all actions and (conclusions) before, during, and after the even. During a traumatic event, it may be essential for self-survival, because of the nature of the event, to separate from others, leave people behind, kill, and/or lie. A person could have violated their personal moral philosophy in order to stay safe, or alive and in doing so they develop guilt over their decisions.

I didn't fight hard enough. . . if I had maybe. . . - Army Veteran.

Avoidance
Most people can understand the need to avoid the perpetrator and the place that the assault happened, but sometimes it does not cease there. When avoidance becomes extreme and the way in which you have coped with the experience, it can become debilitating. You might begin to avoid people all together, fearful they will find out about the trauma, and that they would not be sympathetic to your experience. Avoidance is not only physical, it can also be emotional. You may be emotionally avoiding the thoughts or feelings about the trauma. When you are reminded,

you immediately think about something else, or you numb your emotions (sadness, anger) so that you do not experience the pain. You believe if you allow yourself to feel, you will not be able to handle it, or you will begin to cry and will never stop. This type of avoidance can interfere with reducing symptoms and negatively affect your quality of life.

I use to always go out. . . get all dressed up. . . now I just stay home, no more nights out for me. - Army Veteran.

Just rather not have to answer their (friend's) questions, so I don't return calls or anything else. – Army Veteran, reserve.

She (my wife) shut down completely, she didn't want to talk or anything. – Spouse of Air Force Veteran.

Numbing

Extreme numbness has been described as a shutting down of all emotions relating to trauma and life. In mild form you do not experience emotions about the trauma in general, but can have emotions like anger and sadness about other concerns, however tender affections are usually not felt. You can feel as though you are disconnected from the world and/or your body, or that you are now two people, one which experienced the trauma, and your current conscious self. Things you used to enjoy doing and interests you had no longer have an emotional attachment. Many wonder how they can have no feelings when others around them, family and friends, seem to be experiencing rage, anger, and sadness. When you are emotionally disconnected, you can talk in great detail or write about the trauma without batting an eye. Although this might be interpreted from others, or even yourself, as the experience not being traumatic, or as some might say - not too bad; this is false. Numbing does not mean that you were not traumatized, or that the above list of emotions will not someday leak out or explode.

Emotional numbing may go along with a physical experience of pins and needles, alienation, detachment from others, and/or feelings of being in a dream like state of unreality. Mentally, you can have impaired concentration, paralysis of will, amnesia, inability to plan future action, and/or confusion. An emotionally numb person would have a flat affect. Numb individuals can learn to fake appropriate behavioral responses in social settings in an attempt to mask their inability to feel. Theories behind why a person would become numb, or split in two, has been said to be an initial survival technique. Even at that, continual numbing about the incident is a maladaptive response. You are escaping by altering your state of consciousness, not by dealing with your actions and responses. In your mind events continue to register but they are disconnected from you. It keeps you from being able to healthily integrate the event into yourself.

Sure it (rape) was bad. . . he wouldn't listen when I said no. I have accepted it (only a month ago) and moved on. . . no, I'm not angry, it was just wrong of him to rape me. . . the scars will hardly be noticeable when they are healed. – Marine Corps, Active Duty.

Nightmares

Most of us associate nightmares with childhood dreams of fears about the boogieman, being chased, or monsters under the bed. However, adults can have nightmares, not scary dreams but nightmares; heart-racing, fear-invoking, content which revolves around the trauma. This content tends to be associated around the original threat, or circumstances about the trauma. These nightmares may also have an alternative ending than the original trauma, causing you to question your memory, and/or increase the anxiety originally felt. Upon awaking you typically can remember the nightmare in detail, adding to your already stressful thought patterns. Nightmares can occur more than once during the night, and you may have repeating ones, or repeating themes. Some individuals begin to physically act out in their dreaming state, moving their bodies around, increasing the exhaustion usually associated with continual nightmares. You feel as though you never really slept. If left untreated, these restless nights will drastically begin to affect your daytime behavior. You can become increasingly irritated, tense, doze off, and be unable to concentrate.

My heart felt as though it would jump out of my chest. I stayed awake for the rest of the night. – Army Veteran.

Closing my eyes even scares me now. . . it (nightmare) comes every night. . . too tired in the morning to even think sometimes. – Army, Active Duty.

Flashbacks

Many confuse flashbacks with daymares: a nightmare, which occurs during the daytime. Flashbacks are memories, usually just pieces of your trauma, which encompass any or all of your senses. They are visual, auditory, or tactile, and intrude into your mind without consciously trying to bring them up. These memories can cause a surge of intrusive emotions: anger, confusion, rage, shame, and vulnerability (naming a few), which pull you away from the here and now. Because of the random nature of flashbacks, it can be difficult to make sense of them, or even realize what possibly triggered them in the first place. A sight of a red coat, the smell of a certain perfume, even the small smile of a stranger can trigger a flashback, taking you right back to the time of the trauma; to the emotions of fear, helplessness, and terror, as if you are re-experiencing it all over again. It is not just a thought or memory with no emotions attached. You are actually feeling like you are reliving the trauma; mind, body, and soul.

It (flashback) just happened. I don't have any idea why, I was instantly back there (the assault), not remembering it but there. I can't explain it. Like I was there, my body shook, my face even hurt (she had been hit in the face during the assault). Army Veteran, National Guard.

Spiritual Crisis

Depending on your religious convictions, many have questioned why God allowed this to happen. One might question if there is a Loving God, how could He allow this to happen to you, or why would God want to will this trauma on anyone. We have all been given the agency to choose right or wrong, and in some of the wrong choices, it affects individuals not responsible for that wrongness. In the scriptures, it is written over and over to put your pains and fears into the Lord's hands, and He will carry the burden for you, His sacrifice was sufficient for us all. He understands and knows how to heal our pains so turn your hearts to Him. The Lord never intended anyone to experience abuse so that they could learn some lesson from it. That is not His will; however, if Divine intervention happened every time an innocent person was going to be a victim, then there would be no reason for right and wrong choices, and our agency would be removed. That is also not His plan. Understand this; abuse is wrong and condemned by the Lord.

Forgiveness is a subject many people do not thoroughly understand. It is not denying one's feelings by avoiding the issue. It is Not condoning the act by not seeking legal justice (filing a report, going through with the trial with the purpose of trying to stop him from assaulting anyone else). Holding another person accountable for actions in which they have committed against the law has absolutely nothing to do with forgiveness; just as continuing any relationship with that person, no matter who they are. Once you have forgiven a person, it does not wipe the slate clean to allow any further abuse to yourself or others. You can have already forgiven the perpetrator, and still go forward with legal actions to have that person held accountable for what has been done and to protect others. Forgiveness is you letting go of hate and revengeful thoughts, and trusting in the Lord that no matter the earthly outcome, justice, true justice will always prevail.

Substance Abuse
For many MST survivors, alcohol and drug abuse are frequently comorbid with another mental disorder. A widely theorized reason is that MST survivors are tying to self-medicate their symptoms. Substance abuse is not just abuse of alcohol and drugs. It is a harmful pattern of use of any substance, for mood altering purposes, that advances to frequent and serious problems with work, relationships, and even the law, to name a few. Almost any substance can be abused. Substances such as alcohol and drugs are normally the only ones considered when talking about substance abuse, but cigarettes, caffeine, coffee, prescription medications, over-the-counter medications, food and sugar can also fall under substance abuse. For the best outcome, a mental diagnosis resulting from MST along with substance abuse needs to be treated simultaneously.

Hypervigilance
An increased state of anxiety with a higher state of sensory sensitivity describes hypervigilance. Your behaviors, which can include a high responsiveness to stimuli, unusual increased

arousal, and the constant scanning of the environment, become intensely exaggerated trying to perceive danger. This defense mechanism is an above reasonable checking or watchfulness of one's environment, seemly not in congruence with any type of realistic threat level. It is a response to the unpredictable dangers, which our bodies are watching out for. It can make us cross the street because of a stranger coming toward us, or leave a cart of groceries still in the aisle in reaction to a smile from the person stocking the shelves. It is cumbersome and exhaustive to continually be on the look-out for all possible threats.

Hypervigilance can deprive a person from attending functions because they do not know all the people going and cannot assess all the risks without feeling anxious. They can believe someone is leering at them, judging them, and somehow able to see what they have been through. Depending on where the trauma took place, there can seem to be no safe area to be able to relax, let your guard down, or even just breathe.

Checking them (locks) all of them, ten times, it still does not matter, it's not enough. – Navy Veteran.

(I check the) doors, windows, locks, even the cat door to make sure it is secure. – Marine Corps Veteran.

Suicidal Ideation

Flashbacks are not the only intrusive thought process after your trauma that you could experience. Suicide might be one of those thoughts. All traumas are difficult to get through, but you believe there are circumstances involved in your trauma which may seem to go beyond the ability to continue to live. If you have any of these thoughts, you need to get help now. Continuation of these thoughts usually does not end well. If you are considering suicide and feel unsafe, or if you ever do, you can call the following hotline to speak with someone 24 hours a day who can help: 1-800-273-8255 Press 1, (1-800-273-TALK, Press 1). Or text to 838255. It can be hard to make the call. If you are having trouble, call a good friend who will be able to be with you and help you make that call, but make that call. "The Veterans Crisis Line staff can connect you with VA services to help get your life back on track. Calls can be referred to local Suicide Prevention

Coordinators and other VA providers who specialize in issues such as:

- Post-traumatic stress (PTS/PTSD)
- Traumatic brain injury (TBI)
- Military sexual trauma (MST)
- Family and relationship issues
- Issues related to OEF/OIF/OND deployments

For more information about VA's mental health resources, visit www.mentalhealth.va.gov" (va.gov, 2015).

No, you again, are not going nuts. Your responses, whatever they are, are normal for you. They are normal responses to abnormal events. Taking time to allow yourself to feel the emotions without judging, to understand these responses and be able to identify them, is the beginning. Working through your responses, and integrating them is the next step.

I think about it (suicide) all the time. I thought if I told anyone they would just lock me up so I kept quiet...It felt so good to talk with someone and know I wasn't the only one thinking of it (suicide) and I wasn't locked but I was helped. – Air Force Gulf War Veteran.

Some Vet Centers have specially trained sexual trauma counselors. A list of your local VA facility or Vet Center can be found online at www.va.gov. Also you can call the VA's general information line 1-800-827-1000.

5
STATISTICS

A little bit about understanding statistics, because without knowing the who, what, and how many, percentages are pretty much useless. I loved all my statistic classes, professor's pet all the way. I have always loved numbers and they seemed to come much easier than the complicated and uncanny alphabetical patterns we call the English language. With that said, as you would image, I cringe at many of the reports and "fact sheets" on veterans, especially when it comes to MST. So allow me to open the mind to some of what is just being thrown around. Although it should be straight forward, when looking at data from: reports, surveys, studies, and projections; at times the individuals who are conducting or paying for the data, tend to hide the basic foundation of their information: who, what, where and how many.

The one study which comes to mind, over and over, has been lost (in 2007, I'm still searching for it) in the pile of "did not use" for data, but lingers in small amounts, still hand-written in the margins of another study, was a VA survey conducted to find out why women veterans were not utilizing the VA healthcare services. I had taken all the percentages and the numbers were not adding up. It seemed a majority of women veterans were utilizing the VA healthcare services and the comments were also abnormal. I hunted down all the evidence and the riddle was easily solved. The data was collected from a small (less than 15) amount of women veterans who were waiting for an appointment in a few (I think it was 3) VA medical facilities. Yes, the VA asked women veterans who were already using the VA healthcare services why they were not using the VA healthcare services. After that I was especially careful with all the statistics I encountered. It becomes a game of find the numbers, at times. So, I shall try to not use percentages unless there is something to quantify them with; however, there can be a few percentages just stated because of noteworthiness.

Most of the quotes which use statistical percentages, wording, and numbers were verified; however, if questioning one, the web sites, articles, and books, they are derived from, are listed in the reference section in the back. It would take months to track down all the actual surveys, questionnaires, census, and studies to *maybe* quantify them, and by that time this book would be outdated and I would need to start all over.

How many have experienced sexual assault or sexual harassment? In a study (2001, Sadler et al.) of 537 veteran women, 36% were physically threatened or experienced a completed physical assault while in the military. Also in this study, 79% recounted experiences of sexual harassment; 54% reported unwanted sexual contact; and, of the completed physical assaults, 21% were entirely in the context of rape. Sadler's results (about military risk factors for women: nonfatal assaults) indicated "Workplace violence was a common experience for military women."

A study conducted by the VA, reported that since 2002, (29%) 62,448 women VA patients reported military sexual trauma, which is twice as high as in the civilian population, (17.6%). Another study stated one in seven VA patients (125,000 in total) after returning from duty in Iraq (between years 2001-2007), reported having experienced sexual trauma.

Depending on the population studied and the questions asked, 20% - 75% of military women and 1% - 10% of military men experience MST. The true numbers can be much higher considering sexual assaults and sexual harassment are underreported, some saying by 60%-84%. There does not seem to be any studies which account for all military members (active duty, guard, reserve, and veterans), a distance from the incident (which would give a better account, more are likely to disclose), taken anonymously (to account for fears of telling), who have MST, therefore these numbers listed can only be considered guesstaments, but still considerably alarming.

"VA's national screening program, in which every Veteran seen for health care is asked whether he or she experienced MST, provides data on how common MST is among Veterans seen in VA. National data from this program reveal that about 1 in 4 women and 1 in 100 men respond "yes," that they experienced MST, when screened by their VA provider. Although rates of MST are higher among women, because there are so many more men than women in the military, there are actually significant numbers of women and men seen in VA who have experienced MST.

It's important to keep in mind that these data speak only to the rate of MST among Veterans who have chosen to seek VA health care; they cannot be used to make an estimate of the actual rates of sexual assault and harassment experiences among all individuals serving in the U.S. Military. Also, although Veterans who respond "yes" when screened are asked if they are interested in learning about MST-related services available, not every Veteran who responds "yes" necessarily needs or is interested in treatment. MST is an experience, not a diagnosis, and Veterans' current treatment needs will vary" (mentalhealth.va.gov, 2014).

The VA estimated that some 60,000 to 200,000 women veterans have been sexually assaulted on active duty prior to 1996 (Pardue, Moniz, 1996). Conservatively speaking, since there are over 1,551,710 living veteran women in the US (2013, Census) and approximately 19,694,514 living veteran men in the US (VetPop2014, Veterans Affairs), then between 310,342 (20%) and 667,236 (43%) of veteran women and between 196,946 (1%) and 1,969,452 (10%) of veteran men who are alive living in the US, have experienced Military Sexual Trauma (MST); these numbers are not including veterans outside the US, and members still in the military – active, guard or reserves.

The most recent (which the numbers are in for) Workplace and Gender Relations Survey of Active Duty Members was 2012, by Defense Manpower Data Center (DMDC). The population of interest consisted of:
- Army, Navy, Marine Corps, and Air Force members, excluding National Guard and Reserve members;
- Who had at least six months service at the time the questionnaire was first fielded;
- Were below flag rank.

"Fielding of the survey began September 17, 2012 and ended on November 9, 2012. Completed surveys were received from approximately 23,000 eligible active duty population of 1.35

million" (DoD WGRS, 2012). The listed numbers were 22,792 eligible respondents' completed surveys. Completed counted surveys means that at least 50% or more of the survey was answered. The results were organized into a variety of reporting categories. After respondents were classified by their categories, if the self-reported data was missing, the DMDC's Active Duty Master File (ADMF) was used to credit the subgroup classification at the time of the sampling

The survey asked the participants to respond to each answer by referring to only one incident (the worst) which occurred to them in the past 12 months. Many questions had multiple available answers to an individual question; therefore, adding up some of the answered percentages for a given question can equal more than 100%.

I understand the limitation of doing surveys, even when you have the financial backing of the DoD; however, the description of what was considered "Unwanted Sexual Contact" seemed to blemish the results. Question 32 in the survey reads: "In the past 12 months, have you experienced any of the following intentional sexual contacts that were against your will or occurred when you did not or could not consent where someone…

- Sexually touched you (e.g., intentional touching of genitalia, breasts, or buttocks) or made you sexually touch them?
- Attempted to make you have sexual intercourse, but was not successful?
- Made you have sexual intercourse?
- Attempted to make you perform or receive oral sex, anal sex, or penetration by a finger or object, but was not successful?
- Made you perform or receive oral sex, anal sex, or penetration by a finger or object?"

It would seem straight forward, right? Not exactly. So some guy comes up behind you, makes some disgusting sexual suggestions, grabs you by the arm and you shove him away with the body position that if he tries it again he will get hurt, was it "Unwanted Sexual Contact"? How about your supervisor comes over to your desk and starts to give you an unwanted, unasked for shoulder massage, you cringe, he notices but does not stop for a bit? If I used the definition above I would answer "no." I believe a few extremely essential words were omitted which could make all the difference.

In the Executive Summary, it indicates a little different definition, the "term "unwanted sexual contact" means intentional sexual contact that was against a person's will or which occurred when the person did not or could not consent, and includes completed or attempted sexual intercourse, sodomy (oral or anal sex), penetration by an object, and the unwanted touching of genitalia and other sexually-related areas of the body." Someone seems to have summarized the definition instead of giving what the participant actually read to mean unwanted sexual contact. The writer of this definition, whom more than likely was not "legal counsel" or "expert" seems to have accidentally hit on something that would have been more authentic.

In the Questions Frequently Asked (QFA), under number three it seems to ask the same question, to a degree. The answer to the question was the "definition was created in collaboration with DoD legal counsel and experts in the field to help respondent better relate their experience(s) to the types of sexual assault behaviors addressed by military law and the DoD Sexual Assault Prevention and Response program." Then somebody totally missed that within the UCMJ there is an excellent definition of "sexual contact" that makes it more conducive to what sexual contact and especially unwanted sexual contact is. The part missing from the definition used by DMDC is: "The term 'sexual contact' means—
…(B) any touching, or causing another person to touch, either directly or through the clothing, any body part of any person, if done with an intent to arouse or gratify the sexual desire of any person. Touching may be accomplished by any part of the body" (Article 120, UCMJ).

It may be a little on the wordy side, but I am sure the legal counsel and experts could have incorporate something a little more inclusive of what "sexual contact" really is. The DMDC's definition is more in line with what is considered rape and aggravated sexual assault, but misses a very large percentage of unwanted sexual experiences that in which contact was a part of. Their explanation for the definition "Many respondents cannot and do not consider the complex legal elements of a crime when being victimized by an offender. Consequently, forcing respondent to accurately categorize which offense they experienced would not be productive." What is also not productive is limiting the definition to what a reasonable person would described as rape, attempted rape, or aggravated sexual assault only, leaving out other types of unwanted sexual contact. Although the same definition has been utilized since 2006 to provide DoD with reliable data points across time, it also neglects voluminous unwanted sexual experiences.

Question thirty-three (Q33) had a significantly low response, it seems only 2% (of the participants who answered "yes" to unwanted sexual contact) actually responded to the question "In the past 12 months, how many separate incidents of sexual touching, attempted or completed intercourse, oral or anal sex, or penetration by a finger or object did you experience?" In the report is lists on the survey "[Ask if Q32 = "Yes"], faded out, so it would indicate, since the survey was taken online, that if you answered Q32 "yes", then you would get Q33; however, with many online surveys opposed to paper, where it usually has a prompt if the previous question was answered yes, then answer this question (33), you would automatically know that question 33 referred back to question 32. I did not go through the online questionnaire so this is an assumption; however, it would account for the extremely low response, that participants viewed the question as inappropriately personal and had nothing to do with the subject matter, and not referring directly to Q32, yes to unwanted sexual contact.

Question 92 "[Ask if "Years of Service" >3]" faded, so again it should have populated if the person had been in longer than three (3) years. "92. In your opinion, has *sexual assault* in the military become more or less of a problem over the last 4 years?" Selection for answers: "1. Less of a problem today"; "2. About the same as 4 years ago"; and "3. More of a problem today". (The underlined and italicized words were in the report.) This is where the numbers can be moved around; "Note. Percentage responding are active duty members who answered the question and who had been in active duty service for four years or more, Member's years of service determined by administrative data. NR: Not reportable."

So does that mean the 57% who responded were from the number of the ones who had been in the service longer than 4 years? Or related to the total number in the survey because if not, then you have 57% of an unknown number. This is where the guestimates come in; if I assumed that everyone who was from the grade E-4 and above had service of longer than four years, then the number would be from 18,161 eligible respondents, then 57% (10,351) answered the question. The results:

- 24% (2,484) answered "1. Less of a problem today"
- 44% (4,554) answered "2. About the same as 4 years ago"
- 32% (3,312) answered "3. More of a problem today"

Assuming that the 57% is from the total, so it would be 22,792, but limited to who responded and had service over 4 years. That stated:

- 24% (5,470) answered "1. Less of a problem today"
- 44% (10,029) answered "2. About the same as 4 years ago"
- 32% (7,293) answered "3. More of a problem today"

*Note. When using percentages of percentages the numbers do not always add up to the total amount and the percentages do not always add up to 100%.

It does not seem to make any difference, the percentages are still the same and the statistics can account to projecting the numbers up to be statically significant of the approximately 1,354,883 members on active duty at the time of the survey, with more than 6 months in service. The problem would be if someone did not read the report correctly, retrieved just the numbers and not percentages of answers, then there lies one problem. One could write "out of a survey of about 23,000 military members, (7,293 or 3,312) answered that sexual assault is more of a problem today," one would get a working percentage, the other would be considerably off.

Going back to Q90, I could be writing an article and put, "Although many groups claim there is rampant sexual assault and harassment in the military, within the 2012 WGRA, only 7% of military members state they have had any intentional sexual contacts against their will since they joined the military, and that percentage is significantly lower than the average in the civilian population." What I just did was the apples vs. oranges which comes up in many articles which do not cite where they got their information from (the percentage of civilian intentional sexual contacts against their will), even if the percentage was stated and the source, most do not go and check out the reports. The report could have only been from the FBI who does not use "intentional sexual contacts against the will" for their reporting of any sexually based crime, and that is another limitation, FBI usually reports the number of forcible rapes to women, crimes reported; apples vs. pineapple trees. It sometimes all depends on how the writer wants to use or compare different stats.

Out of the entire survey, the one question which I believe is key is Q90. If the answer to Q32 (unwanted sexual contact) was "no" then this question would populate because the "yes" answers to Q32 would already be added and there would be no need for redundancy. "90. <u>Since the date you first joined the military</u>, have you ever experienced any of the following intentional sexual contacts that were <u>against your will or occurred when you did not or could not consent</u> where someone…

- <u>Sexually</u> *touched you* (e.g., intentional touching of genitalia, breasts, or buttocks) or made you sexually touch them?
- <u>Attempted</u> to make you have sexual intercourse, but was not successful?
- <u>Made</u> you have sexual intercourse?
- <u>Attempted</u> to make you perform or receive oral sex, anal sex, or penetration by a finger or object, but was not successful?
- <u>Made</u> you perform or receive oral sex, anal sex, or penetration by a finger or object?"

For Q90, 7% (1,596) of all the (22,792) respondents selected "Yes." From all of the percentages tossed around about sexual assault and harassment this number seems low; however, breaking it down, out of the (11,553) "Females," 23% (2658) indicated "Yes," and out of the (11,239) "Males," 4% (450) indicated "Yes," which is more in line with the bulk of other studies.

To be as prudent as possible, making sure the numbers match what the result state, it is much easier to just regurgitate the information and allow the reader to extract what they need…

LAST YEAR'S KEY FINDINGS – FY 2012 (OCTOBER 1, 2011
THROUGH SEPTEMBER 30, 2012)
- Reports of Sexual Assault
--Reports of sexual assault increased in three of four Military
Services. In total, the DoD received 3,374 reports of sexual
assault involving one or more Service members as either the
victim or alleged subject (suspect) – a five percent increase over
the 3,192 reports of received in FY11.
  - Of the 3,374 reports, about 60 percent involved Service
    member-on-Service member crime.
  - The 3,374 reports involved 2,828 Service member victims
    making a report for an incident that occurred while they
    were in military service.
--Of the 3,374 reports in FY12, 2,558 were Unrestricted Reports
and 816 remained Restricted at the end of the year.
--Approximately four percent of the 3,374 reports of sexual
assault were for sexual assault incidents that occurred prior to a
member's military service.
  - Estimated Past-Year Prevalence of Sexual Assault
--Of those surveyed, 6.1 percent of Active Duty women and 1.2
percent of Active Duty men indicated experiencing unwanted
sexual contact (USC) in the 12 months prior to being surveyed.
These prevalence rates indicate that approximately 26,000
Active Duty members experienced some form of USC in the
year prior to being surveyed.
  - Of the 6.1 percent of Active Duty women surveyed who
    indicated experiencing USC: 31 percent reported a
    completed penetration, 26 percent reported attempted
    penetration, 32 percent reported unwanted sexual touching,
    and 10 percent did not specify the USC experienced.
  - Of the 1.2 percent of Active Duty men surveyed who
    indicated experiencing USC: 10 percent reported a
    completed penetration, 5 percent reported attempted
    penetration, 51 percent reported unwanted sexual touching,
    and 34 percent did not specify the USC experienced.

- Command Action
  --Of the 2,661 subjects with case dispositions reported in FY12, the Department had legal authority over 1,714 (64 percent) of them.
  --Of the 1,714 Service member cases considered by convening authorities, sufficient evidence existed to take some kind of action against 1,124 of them (66 percent). This action could have been for a sexual assault crime or any other misconduct identified during the criminal investigation.
  --Of the 880 subjects who received action on a sexual assault offense:
    - 68 percent had court-martial charges preferred (initiated)
    - 18 percent were entered into nonjudicial punishment proceedings under Article 15, Uniform Code of Military Justice (UCMJ)
    - 15 percent received an adverse administrative action or discharge

THIS YEAR'S KEY FINDINGS – FY 2013 (OCTOBER 1, 2012 THROUGH SEPTEMBER 30, 2013)
  - Reports of Sexual Assault
    --Reports of alleged sexual assault increased in all four Military Services. In total, the DoD received 5,061 reports of alleged sexual assault involving one or more Service members as either the victim or alleged subject (suspect) – a 50 percent increase over the 3,374 reports of received in FY12.
      - Of the 5,061 reports, about 54 percent involved Service member-on-Service member crime.
      - The 5,061 reports involved 4,113 Service member victims making a report for an incident that occurred while they were in military service.
    --Of the 5,061 reports in FY13, 3,768 were Unrestricted Reports and 1,293 remained Restricted at the end of the year.
    --Approximately 10 percent of the 5,061 reports of sexual assault were for sexual assault incidents that occurred prior to a member's military service.

- Estimated Past-Year Prevalence of Sexual Assault
  --No USC rate is available, as no survey was conducted during this fiscal year. A survey is being fielded in 2014 to update past-year prevalence rates of USC and sexual harassment.
- Command Action
  --Of the 3,234 subjects with case dispositions reported in FY13, the Department had legal authority over 2,149 (66 percent) of them.
  --Of the 2,149 Service member cases considered by convening authorities for action, sufficient evidence existed to take some kind of action against 1,569 of them (73 percent). This action could have been for a sexual assault crime or any other misconduct identified during the criminal investigation.
  --Of the 1,187 subjects who received action on a sexual assault offense:
    - 71 percent had court-martial charges preferred (initiated)
    - 18 percent were entered into nonjudicial punishment proceedings under Article 15, UCMJ
    - 12 percent received an adverse administrative action or discharge.

6
MENTAL HEALTH

Therapist

The decision to talk with a therapist about the intrusive thoughts, nightmares, and/or anger issues, no matter what the concern, should not have an ounce of shame, embarrassment, or disgrace attached to it. Seeking help is courageous, commendable, and respectable. Although much stigma is attached to requesting to see a therapist, it is considerably healthier than trying to muddle through on your own. The detestable statement, "It's all in your head," heard over and over by many survivors, should not interfere with continuing the search for help. In recent studies, victims of traumatic stress actually experience physical changes to the hippocampus (a part of the brain). Extreme stress can have lasting effects on many parts of the brain, and there is research as well as many books providing more information about additional physical consequences to the brain from stress.

The decision on which therapist, and/or therapy you agree to is a very formidable one, and not to be taken lightly. Choosing a therapist and the type of therapy you will feel comfortable with is not as easy as it might first seem. The specialized techniques utilized by psychotherapy can produce lasting changes in your life, even if they are profound and long-term problems. Not all therapists/counselors prescribe to the same types of therapy, and there is a very big difference in the various therapies. Constructing a relationship of trust with the therapist can lead to restructuring significant emotional experiences; therefore the alliance you establish with the therapist is the foundation for therapy. This relationship is crucial to working through your traumatic experiences, hopefully resulting in lessening of symptoms and bringing functionability back into your life.

The credentialing of therapists is exceptionally confusing. There are hundreds of designations and you quickly feel as though you are in alphabet soup (LCSW, LPC, MFT, MD, Psy.D, to name a few). Therapists can be certified, licensed, and registered from various authorities, with particular modalities: cognitive behavioral; psychodynamic; psychoanalytic; and more. Deciphering which therapy can be daunting; yet, there have been studies on therapies particularly designed to help PTSD and other diagnoses resulting from sexual trauma(s).

Have you ever just met someone and knew you would be great friends or that you just do not click? These unconscious messages are real and should be listened to. They are communications from you to yourself. Learning how to utilize these unconscious messages to your advantage can be tricky. Many times your conscious and unconscious mind seems to disagree. Using these unconscious pieces of information through feelings, responses and sometimes dreams, to evaluate the successfulness of the particular therapist and therapy, is a constructive asset. Do not disregard gut feelings, but utilize them with your other tools, in selecting the right therapist and therapy for you.

Privacy is an important aspect of your therapy. You have the right to complete privacy during your sessions as well as absolute confidentiality. Nobody should be able to listen in on your sessions; directly or indirectly. Your therapist should not be discussing any aspect of the sessions or you with anyone else, without your written consent. All information should stay in your file unless you authorize otherwise, and you should know exactly what information will be shared if you do give consent. There are other aspects to privacy outside the therapy session which also should be noted. Having to continually schedule your appointments with the secretary, or sitting in the waiting room with another client for a long period of time is unnerving, unnecessary and not private.

A safe environment for therapy encompasses the whole environment, extending beyond the room. It incorporates the first initial contact with the therapist and her/his office; scheduling; fees; your records and more. If at any time during the process you feel uneasy about anything, it needs to be addressed. Allowing such troubled thoughts to continue while in therapy can cause unconstructive distress that will hamper the ability for you to freely unveil your issues.

For many consistency is essential in therapy. Meeting at the same place, same time, same day of the week, with the same session length, creates consistency and stability in the details, allowing you to release the pain in a secure and safe framework. With this said, the VA system is not what I have just listed. There is a serious lack in the Mental Health section of the VA for qualified therapist, not social workers, therapist (there is a difference); however, there also is not many social workers. There is usually not an ability to see a therapist at the same time, for the amount the veteran needs. I have been in and out of the "scheduling system," for lack of a better description, because someone somewhere canceled one of my appointments and did not think to make another one at that time. I canceled an appointment and was told that another would be scheduled for me (it was not); changing of schedulers and out I was again. Then there is the "I don't know what happened" statement when I questioned why I have not gotten an appointment in awhile, even though in my records the therapist has listed when she would like to have me scheduled again, and finally I get back into the scheduling.

There are certain items to keep in mind when selecting a therapist:
- Make sure you are not pushed into selecting the therapist by anyone; friend, family member or another healthcare provider.
- Make sure the therapist is not seeing someone you know.
- The therapist should not be related to you, a friend, the relative of a friend, or even the friend of a friend.
- In selecting a therapist, remove any person who can be connected to you in any way other than as your therapist.
- Make sure your therapist does not socialize in the same circles you do. Occasionally bumping into her/him outside the office is fine, but having many encounters could cause unnecessary nervousness.
- A respectable therapist begins with a Master's or Doctorate degree in a mental health field.
- After the completion of a degree by a credible school, the therapist needs to have clinical residency in psychotherapy.
- Academic degrees or licensures are not stamps of approval or competency for a therapist. You should find out as much as you can about them.

There are a few red flags, which once raised, the thought of discontinuing with your therapist should be in your mind:

- If the therapist answers the phone while in session.
- If the therapist talks to you while in session with another person.
- If you ever hear the therapist talk about another client (sometimes the therapist might say they had a client that did that too, but this is not what I am referring to) where you would be able to know who they are.
- If you are continually asked to confirm your appointments with the therapist's secretary after they have already been made (not to include the "efficient" VA system).
- If the therapist is continually late.
- If the therapist continually cancels appointments (not the computer, or other viral VA computer system ghosts).
- If the therapist allows your session time to frequently go over into another's time.
- If the session time of the client before you continues to go into your session time.
- If you are privy to another client's confidential information.

The VA staffs many credentialed counselors, but unfortunately not all facilities have a therapist, and many are not women. The VA does authorize what in the past was called "fee-base:" paying an outside agency (a therapist in the community) for services which that particular VA facility does not offer. "The Non-VA Medical Care program provides payment authorization for eligible Veterans to obtain routine outpatient or inpatient medical services through community providers. The authorization may be granted when it has been determined that direct VA services are either geographically inaccessible or VA facilities are not available to meet a Veteran's needs. All community services must be preapproved before a Veteran receives treatment. However, it may not be possible to contact VA prior to treatment in emergency situations. Each individual Veteran's eligibility status and medical care needs are reviewed to decide whether payment for community treatment can be approved. The VA also requires a 72-hour notification of emergency room care" (va.gov, 2015). Check with the VA facilities' MST Coordinator for more information. One aspect to always remember, you do NOT have to accept any therapist. If you do not feel safe with her/him, you do not want to waste your or their time, but more importantly you do not need any more anxiety in your life.

Diagnosis

There is not a designated point at which you will receive a diagnosis for your symptoms. It can occur prior to starting therapy by a referral from a medical doctor, after discussing your issues with a therapist, or not at all. Many therapists offer their professional opinion accompanied by the DSM-V (Diagnostic and Statistical Manual of Mental Disorders) to propose a diagnosis. Therapy is one method for relieving the symptoms. Medication and medication with therapy are two others. Although the DSM-V has specific criteria for every diagnosis, there are many overlaps in some categories, which can cause a misdiagnosis.

The complexities in diagnosing an individual are diverse, and a misdiagnosis can be the result of certain criteria not being disclosed to the therapist. "The Diagnostic and Statistical Manual of Mental Disorders (DSM) is the standard classification of mental disorders used by mental health professionals in the United States. It is intended to be applicable in a wide array of contexts and used by clinicians and researchers of many different orientations (e.g., biological, psychodynamic, cognitive, behavioral, interpersonal, family/systems). The Diagnostic and Statistical Manual of Mental Disorders, Fifth Edition (DSM-5) is the current edition and has been designed for use across clinical settings (inpatient, outpatient, partial hospital, consultation-liaison, clinic, private practice, and primary care), with community populations. It can be used by a wide range of health and mental health professionals, including psychiatrists and other physicians, psychologists, social workers, nurses, occupational and rehabilitation therapists, and counselors. It is also a necessary tool for collecting and communicating accurate public health statistics" (2013, APA).

Misdiagnoses occur more often than many think, and more often than others deem necessary. The crossover of criteria from one disorder to another can cause more complications than just a mere misdiagnosis. Numerous factors figure into the identification: from a patient's physical and medical history, to his/her current and previous symptomologies, as well as personal and family mental health history. The therapist progresses throughout the DSM-V exploring all bases. A key component in discovering the underlined difficulties leading to a proper diagnosis is the disclosing of valuable information of mental/physical history and current symptoms from the survivor. Numerous survivors understandably possess a lack of trust, even toward the therapist, making it difficult to disclose their personal information, which can become a source for escorting them both down a mistaken path.

Joining the military (for women) increases the risk factor of being sexually assaulted; having experienced MST *radically* increases the likelihood of developing PTSD.

Reading through the criteria of disorders in the DSM-V, countless MST survivors find their symptoms mirrored on many pages; however, one very relevant criterion is the trauma itself. If the altering point of your "then" reactions (feeling normal) to the "current" ones (uncharacteristic of who you were) is the traumatic event, then PTSD seems to be the best diagnosis for MST survivors whose symptoms are within the specific criteria. Another contributing factor for MST survivors is patient disclosure. MST survivors usually have trust issues, and disclosing of information, even valuable information necessary for a competent diagnosis can come slowly and with difficulty, causing multiple diagnoses.

> *Military sexual assault (sexual assault experienced while in military service) is an additional traumatic stressor that affects military personnel, and subsequently, is identified as an exposure leading to PTSD in some, generally female, veterans. There is evidence that military sexual assault makes PTSD more likely than similar assault before or after military service, increases the likelihood of developing PTSD (Committee on Treatment of Posttraumatic Stress Disorder, 2007).*

The term comorbidity refers to having more than one disorder. Because a person has been diagnosed with one mental disorder, does not preclude all others, as numerous people can have more than one diagnosed mental disorder. Comorbidity can lead one evaluator to affirm one diagnosis while another evaluator gives another. This dual (or more) diagnosis does not constitute misdiagnosis, but reveals the complexity of a person's potential life experiences, and possible genetic mental maladjustments.

Once a person has been diagnosed with a mental disorder, it is advantageous to research the particular disorder; comprehending the criteria, and understand the reasons behind the decision. Any therapist should be able to discuss their rational for assigning that particular disorder. This is not an attempt to question the diagnosis, or the therapist, but enhance the patient's ability to assist in their own therapy.

Posttraumatic Stress Disorder

In 2013, the American Psychiatric Association revised the PTSD diagnostic criteria in the fifth edition of its Diagnostic and Statistical Manual of Mental Disorder (DSM-5).

A major change has happened with the publication of the DSM-V (2013), to the criteria for PTSD. There are now four major clusters – reexperiencing the event; heightened arousal; negative thoughts and mood or feelings. "DSM-5 criteria for posttraumatic stress disorder differ significantly from those in DSM-IV. As described previously for acute stress disorder, the stressor criterion (Criteria A) is more explicit with regard to how an individual experienced "traumatic" events. Also, Criterion A2 (subject reaction) has been eliminated. Whereas there were three major symptoms clusters in DMS-IV –reexperiencing, avoidance/numbing cluster is divided into two distinct clusters: avoidance and persistent negative alterations in cognitions and mood. This latter category, which retains most of the DSM-IV numbing symptoms, also new or reconceptualized symptoms, such as persistent negative emotional states. The final cluster – alterations in arousal and reactivity –retains most of the DSM-IV arousal symptoms. It also includes irritable or aggressive behavior and reckless or self-destructive behavior."

There is nothing wrong with having PTSD, and it is better to be diagnosed with it (when you have it) than to continue having it disrupt your life. Diagnostic criteria for PTSD include a history of exposure to a traumatic event that meets specific stipulations and symptoms from each of four symptom clusters: intrusion, avoidance, negative alterations in cognitions and mood, and alterations in arousal and reactivity. The sixth criterion concerns duration of symptoms; the seventh assesses functioning; and, the eighth criterion clarifies symptoms as not attributable to a substance or co-occurring medical condition.

Two specifications are noted including delayed expression and a dissociative subtype of PTSD, the latter of which is new to DSM-5. In both specifications, the full diagnostic criteria for PTSD must be met for application to be warranted.

Criterion A: stressor
The person was exposed to: death, threatened death, actual or threatened serious injury, or actual or threatened sexual violence, as follows: (**one required**)
1. Direct exposure.
2. Witnessing, in person.
3. Indirectly, by learning that a close relative or close friend was exposed to trauma. If the event involved actual or threatened death, it must have been violent or accidental.
4. Repeated or extreme indirect exposure to aversive details of the event(s), usually in the course of professional duties (e.g., first responders, collecting body parts; professionals repeatedly exposed to details of child abuse). This does not include indirect non-professional exposure through electronic media, television, movies, or pictures.

Criterion B: intrusion symptoms
The traumatic event is persistently re-experienced in the following way(s): (**one required**)
1. Recurrent, involuntary, and intrusive memories.
2. Traumatic nightmares.
3. Dissociative reactions (e.g., flashbacks) which may occur on a continuum from brief episodes to complete loss of consciousness.
4. Intense or prolonged distress after exposure to traumatic reminders.
5. Marked physiologic reactivity after exposure to trauma-related stimuli.

Criterion C: avoidance
Persistent effortful avoidance of distressing trauma-related stimuli after the event: (**one required**)
1. Trauma-related thoughts or feelings.
2. Trauma-related external reminders (e.g., people, places, conversations, activities, objects, or situations).

Criterion D: negative alterations in cognitions and mood
Negative alterations in cognitions and mood that began or worsened after the traumatic event: (**two required**)
1. Inability to recall key features of the traumatic event (usually dissociative amnesia; not due to head injury, alcohol, or drugs).
2. Persistent (and often distorted) negative beliefs and expectations about oneself or the world (e.g., "I am bad," "The world is completely dangerous").
3. Persistent distorted blame of self or others for causing the traumatic event or for resulting consequences.
4. Persistent negative trauma-related emotions (e.g., fear, horror, anger, guilt, or shame).
5. Markedly diminished interest in (pre-traumatic) significant activities.
6. Feeling alienated from others (e.g., detachment or estrangement).
7. Constricted affect: persistent inability to experience positive emotions.

Criterion E: alterations in arousal and reactivity
Trauma-related alterations in arousal and reactivity that began or worsened after the traumatic event: (**two required**)
1. Irritable or aggressive behavior
2. Self-destructive or reckless behavior
3. Hypervigilance
4. Exaggerated startle response
5. Problems in concentration
6. Sleep disturbance

Criterion F: duration
Persistence of symptoms (in Criteria B, C, D, and E) for more than one month.

Criterion G: functional significance
Significant symptom-related distress or functional impairment (e.g., social, occupational).

Criterion H: exclusion
Disturbance is not due to medication, substance use, or other illness (ptsd.va.gov, 2015).

Major Depression

Just as with PTSD, there is a set of check-listed criteria for Major Depression and a mental health professional needs to diagnose you. The DSM-V leaves Major Depression alone for criteria; however, the bereavement exclusion has been removed. During a specific amount of time, you are generally depressed for most of the day, nearly every day and/or have a loss of interest or pleasure. The diagnoses further lists what symptoms are displayed, such as: depressed mood, loss of interest/pleasure, weight loss/increase, decrease or increase in appetite, not being able to fall/stay asleep, thoughts of worthlessness; agitation; loss of energy, lack of concentration, suicidal ideation, thinking a lot about death, and an inability to focus. This list is not all inclusive and your symptoms can come and go (episodes), but it is not just feeling sad.

Some MST survivors have been diagnosed with Borderline Personality Disorder (BPD) - because of unknown biological factors and invalidating environments during childhood the person reacts excessively to emotional stimulation. Their emotions shift rapidly in extremes. People and objects to them are all good or all bad. They live crisis-dappled lives, which are pervasive and cross a broad range of personal and social situations, and the "onset can be traced back to at least adolescence or early adulthood" (DSM-IV, 2000). The functionability (or better stated unfunctionability) of a person with BPD would not at all be cohesive with any military environment, and they most likely would not have been able to graduate from Boot Camp, or have any significant amount of time in service. A BPD diagnosis is not a cause and effect relationship to MST; a traumatic event is not a criterion for the disorder.

Many question if they are receiving therapy or therapy and medication, which is decreasing many of the symptoms resulting from experiencing MST, why persist in questioning a diagnosis? Certain mental disorders are classified (by VA and Armed Forces) as pre-existing to joining the military, or genetic and not due to service. When given such a label, it can create difficulties acquiring services and benefits from the VA, and a military member can be discharged for it. Even with the opening of treatments and services for a survivor of MST, the condition for which services are being sought must be related to the MST (when the veteran is not already receiving VA services). Because of these preconditions, they are generally not considered service connected. If it was, the veteran must establish the prior disorder was aggravated or worsened by military service, which can be problematic to accomplish. Complicating the matter, when seeking veterans' disability benefits with these diagnosed personality disorders, another disorder with similar criteria (classified as possibly service-connected) could be over looked.

Therapy

Therapy -
1. The treatment of disease or disorders, as by some
remedial, rehabilitating, or curative process: speech therapy.
2. A curative power or quality.
3. Psychotherapy.
4. Any act, hobby, task, program, etc., that relieves tension.

No two people are the same, just as no two sexual assaults, even if the victim or perpetrator are the same; therefore, it is absurd to believe all military sexual trauma victims will benefit from just one modality of therapy. One way to determine which therapy could help to reduce negative symptoms and be able to positively cope with automatic reactions is to create a list of ten, investigate what each entails and eliminate ones you have absolutely no faith in or seem wacked. Make a list of the possibilities combined with the ones not dejected and you have a sincere beginning at which to start. Understand most therapist employ more than one type of therapy, just as you can select more than one. There are numerous positive elements associated with the diversity of therapies, which hopefully will help in the healing process.

If you are a veteran, VA provides free confidential counseling and treatment for physical and mental conditions related to MST experiences. A veteran does not need to be service connected, and may be able to receive the counseling and treatment even if they otherwise are not eligible for other VA care. Evidence of, reporting of the incident(s), or military documenting the trauma occurred, is not necessary. If you are already seeking medical care at a VA facility, speak to your primary health care provider (va.gov, 2015).

There is supposed to be a designated MST Coordinator at every VA facility and a contact person for all MST-related issues. This coordinator is the advocate for finding and accessing community resources, state and federal benefits, and VA services and programs.

> *Any veteran who believes he/she experienced MST can apply... for counseling and treatment of any MST-related injury, illness, or psychological condition, without obligation for co-payment. Veterans do not need to have a service-connected (sc) rating to receive these services. Even veterans with less than 24 months of active duty service (who otherwise would not be eligible for VA services) are eligible to receive this particular benefit (Boston, 2004).*

Military Sexual Trauma is determined by the statement of the veteran declaring they experienced MST. Eligibility for services is determined by the VA clinician, who determines which problems are related to the MST, other than therapy. It can be seen as admirable that the VA allows the receiving of free counseling and/or medical care for problems associated with experiencing MST; however, a medical clinician will establish what is and is not linked. Nobody can totally determine to an exact point what physical and mental conditions do and do not relate to MST. Because of such, it is advantageous to proceed to a disability claim when the symptoms of experiencing MST interrupt your daily life.

*Psychotherapy - the treatment of psychological
disorders or maladjustments by a professional technique,
as psychoanalysis, group therapy, or behavioral therapy
(dictionary.com, 2013).*

Cognitive Behavior Therapy (CBT) generally seeks to identify harmful thought(s) and thought patterns with the intent of changing/influencing destructive pessimistic emotions and dysfunctional behaviors. It is a collaborative effort between the therapist and client; the therapist listens then encouragingly teaches the client ways in which to unlearn the maladaptive emotions and behaviors. CBT is based on the idea that our thoughts cause our feelings and behaviors, not external conditions, and that we can change the way we think/feel even if the situation does not change. CBT is said (generally) to be the most rapid in terms of results, with a time-limit (session limited) process, highly instructive and giving the client homework.

Dialectical Behavioral Therapy (DBT) mainly utilized for Borderline Personality Disorders, is interested in: first, reducing self-injuring and self-threatening behaviors; then reducing behaviors which interfere with the therapy process; eventually decreasing behaviors that diminish the client's quality of life.

Rational Emotive Behavior Therapy (REBT) views people as prone to embracing irrational beliefs and behaviors, which stand in the way of them accomplishing their purposes and goals. These irrational attitudes take on extreme positions that contrast to healthy rational and flexible wants and desires of the person. The primary focus is on the present and not past trauma(s), and that we do not have to allow the past to influence the way we view the present.

Stress Inoculation Training has three components to the method: education, skill building and application. SIT is an anxiety management treatment therapy utilized generally to treat the fear and anxiety symptoms. SIT is also a time-limited therapy with usually 10-14 sessions where the therapist will educate the client on: identifying cues in the environment which trigger responses; how fear develops as a learned response to trauma; and relaxation exercises. In the skills building segment, the therapist helps the client learn how to control their emotional reactions, and is intended to reduce negative thoughts and physiological sensations. The client then applies the skills learned in managing their response to stimuli and their anxiety symptoms.

Prolonged Exposure Therapy (PE) is based on the concept that we can get used to things that are just annoying and not truly life-threatening or dangerous. With PE, the therapist asks the client to confront the very situations, people, memories, and objects which are attached to the trauma, but conducted in a safe method. It can be done with in vivo (real life), like going to the local park where the trauma occurred, or is associated with imagining you are in the park. PE deems that avoidance of the discomfort reinforces avoidance as a coping skill, and increases the likelihood the anxiety might spread to other aspects of the person's life. Continuation of the exposure is essential to reducing the frequency and severity of the symptoms. This form of therapy can be very emotionally painful for survivors and is not used for every client.

Pharmacotherapy. The symptoms from experiencing MST can become so debilitating that psychotherapy cannot adequately begin without pharmacotherapy (medication). Taking medications is not pathetic. For certain intense symptoms, it is necessary. These medications need not be thought of as a cure-all but as a helper to reduce the issues standing in the way of psychotherapy. Even though a medication is proposed, do not just take it without consideration of the possible benefits and possible harm (side effects) it can do. The benefits to accepting the medication can be: fast working; treat coexisting disorders; stop the escalation of a crisis situation; and (but not limited to) allow you to function until the next therapeutic session. Some of the dilemmas to accepting these medications are: some cause serious medical side effects; dependency on the medication; lead to a denial there is something wrong; causing more symptoms; and sometimes they just do not work (causing more anxiety). Understanding all the implications to taking a prescribed medication is in your best interest. Sometimes the side effects of the medications are worse than the symptoms you are taking them for and will likely focus on just one symptom.

Alternative Therapy

The term alternative therapies is not used to suggest there has not been empirical research conducted but that it is not considered mainstream in medical and clinical realms. Some therapies have been listed in the "alternative therapy" section for years until studies and other empirical data could be collected and that therapy moved to commonly accepted and practiced methodologies.

Acupressure is the process of using finger pressure on specific points on the body.

Acupuncture is the process of using needles (small fine needles), which are inserted at specific points on the body to restore a vital energy balance.

Aromatherapy is the utilization of essential oils, which can be, massaged into the skin, inhaled or added to water (baths, soaking of a specific part of the body), commonly in a diluted manner.

Bibliotherapy uses the connection the client has with selected written works (books, poems, papers) to assist in solving problems and is often combined with writing therapy. Within the context of the written work, the individual can: see themselves; relate to the experience; discover personal negative behaviors; connect with any of the characters; experience emotional happiness all with the understanding that it will be a positive in the client's life.

Biofeedback employs the use of machinery to monitor the individual's metabolic system, having the ability in real time to view the changes and modify them to a poised internal state. The client learns to recognize when their system is negatively responding to a word, memory, picture, etc, and then with the assistance of the therapist, can alter them accordingly.

Emotional Freedom Technique (Tapping Therapy) is a subset of Meridian Tapping Technique. In describing it in its simplest form, it is tapping on certain acupressure points while focusing on a behavior, feeling and/or thought, and that negative feeling, thought and/or behavior is allowed to flow beyond its stuck points.

Eye Movement Desensitization and Reprocessing (EMDR) contains many aspects of different modalities: interpersonal, cognitive behavioral, psychodynamic and body-centered. In the process, the therapist asks the client to focus on a thought or picture (in the mind), then uses an apparatus (finger, pen, light dot) to have the patient follow with their eyes back and forth. After an amount of time, the eye movement is halted and the therapist inquires as to what thoughts, visions etc. has come up. Investigation into that feeling, thought, memory, etc. proceeds or can be the focus and the eye movement begins again. The element used is dual stimulation: bilateral eye movements and tones or taps while the client attends to memories, present triggers, or future experiences. The client begins to replace the negative beliefs with positive ones (which were discussed previous to the session). The duality initiates the emergence of insight, new associations and/or changes in memories. The process is repeated several times while the therapist allows the client to work through their own stuck issues.

Herbalism employs the use of plants or plant-based substances to aid in whatever ailment the person is having.

Homoeopathy is a medical system which draws on the theory that like treats like. A remedy is a minute diluted dose of a natural substance (sometime diluted to the extreme), which if taken in larger doses, would cause the same (like) symptoms. Unlike Herbalism, it makes use of natural plants, animals and minerals.

Hypnotherapy prescribes to the thought that it sometimes is necessary to bypass the conscious mind, and enter the unconscious, where repressed emotions, repressed memories and lost experiences (events), are recorded. Some believe that the unconscious mind can receive suggestive thoughts to change behavior, attitudes, and/or emotions which the conscious mind would reject or have difficulty in facilitating.

Laugh Therapy does sound pretty funny (yes I shall keep my day job), but laughing actually does boost your immune system, reduce stress, lower your blood pressure and increases the use of many muscles. "Of all days, the day on which one has not laughed is the one most surely wasted" (Nicolas Chamfort).

Massage Therapy is a very broad term used to describe multiple styles of physical manipulation of muscles, tendons, ligaments of the topical skin and connective tissues (soft body tissue).

Pet Assisted Therapy is the utilization of trained animals to improve the mental and/or physical health of a person. Even though we had pets from the beginning of human kind, it is only until recently that pets have been accepted by the mainstream, to be trained to assist in the mental and physical health of individuals. What may come to the mind of most people would be guide dogs for the blind. Although they were instituted primarily for a set of second eyes, studies have found the people who had these guide dogs lived longer, did not have as many ailments, and other such positive side-effects of dog ownership. There are trained therapy animals, which help with all kinds of difficulties, some being the detection of an anxiety attack, early detection of a seizure, as visitors in children's wards, in a therapist' office to help overcome some of the difficulties which can occur when having children as clients, and other such methods.

A therapist can utilize just one of the above listed types of therapy or a mixture of two or more compatible ones to target the whole of a person. If you have researched a therapy which you believe could be a helpful addition to the one you already have chosen, discuss this with your therapist and you might open their eyes to a new method. Many of the therapies do not require a licensed therapist to be the facilitator of; however, it is advantageous for survivors of MST to seek out a therapy or combination of therapeutic techniques, which does include a licensed counselor, in the beginning, to provide amble professional help.

Once again the above listed therapies are not even close to a comprehensive list or description of them; no endorsement is made in the inclusion or exclusion for them into this book. Warning: you can certainly find quacks in conventional therapies as well as alternative therapies, so make inquires, investigate and explore any modality you are thinking about. Any form of therapy which actually improves a client's functionability, decreases the suffering, and does not further wound, is worthy to consider; but just as with the diagnosis, knowledge is power, and I cannot advocate enough to investigate all possible avenues before selecting one.

The Community and MST Survivors

There seems to be hundreds of non-profits and other community organizations who have rallied the cry for help to the veteran community. It is mindboggling determining which organization actually helps the veteran, and which ones do not. Prior to volunteering to help or be a participant in any program do a little research. There are many well-intended organizations which forgot their brains when designing programs to help veterans, especially veterans who have experienced Military Sexual Trauma. One in point was a non-profit which thought, or really did not think through, the name of their program to help women MST survivors. They used Athena, who punished Medusa for being raped in her temple, for the program name. I guess it was not that big of an issue for them since after several emails about how inappropriate the name was, it still stood for quite awhile. They were not the only ones, this organization received grant money from a major veterans organization with the name proudly displayed on the grant award site. I had also sent off emails to them, without any response. I guess offending hundreds of thousands of MST survivors was not all that distressing to them.

Other non-profits which promote their help to "wounded warriors," need to be carefully examined also. The term "wounded warrior" has been around long before 9/11, so it really vexes me everytime I see the term "wounded warrior" portraying only veterans who were in after 9/11, as if all the rest of us who were on battlefields and came home injured are not. It would be honorable if non-profits who help only Post-9/11 veterans used Post 9/11 wounded warrior slogans, or made statements which made it clear that is their intended focus. And these same non-profits should not utilize songs which suggest veterans of other conflicts are included in their programs, when they are not, it is deceptive and can only be systemically structured to acquire funds from individuals who believe they are giving to all wounded warriors of all conflicts. The greatest casualty is forgetting the rest of us veterans.

In the past twenty years I have seen programs come and go to "help" MST survivors. Many of them were from the VA and monumental failures. Some from meaningful uneducated non-profits or community based mental health organizations, to which I always wondered why the veteran, who they were wanting so badly to help, was never asked what would help them. Just because a person does not have a degree or is accredited in some area, does not mean they do not know much of what can and what cannot help them. From the beginning I was very skeptical of any VA programs, and I am thankful and not on a mental ward somewhere, because of it. There has been far too much harm done to hundreds (if not thousands) of MST survivors from all of these "helping" programs. So before you step into the room, or fly off to the retreat, do a little ground work, sometimes the help you are given does more damage.

I have been asked some of the most insensitive questions about being assaulted, many by those who are "helping." Along with questions, many of the statements which have come from VA therapists have been just as thoughtless. When I first began to ask for help from the VA, most of the statements were: it could not have happened the way I was telling it, there must be something biologically wrong and not from the traumas, did I really believe that was what I had felt, and it just goes downhill from there. My first experience with non-profits did not go so well either. Tailhook had just hit the media, so now all the letters that I had been writing were getting some response (prior I got nothing). A national organization for women found me and it seemed as though they really wanted to help, they wanted to bring to light the assaults and harassment which was occurring in the militaries. A press conference was set up and I was in front of cameras, journalists, and others (all in the big city, where I traveled to do this). I was going over what I was going to say when a question arose and I said my feelings. I was told that I should not say that, I should say something else. I did not understand, why would they want me to not tell the truth? Well I did not listen to them, I answered the questions and gave a small story line of what I had been through. That was it, they did not even stay after to see if I was ok. I had the first taste of what I still see today, other agendas becoming entangled with support for MST survivors and focus taken away from what the militaries are and are not doing about the continuation of abuse. I have very basic and to the point beliefs, but when talking about MST, that is what I focus on. This has caused, and still does, me being ostracized from many non-profits which claim their focus is on sexual assault and harassment. I have come to terms with it, and I am not about to deny who I am, or what I believe, then, or now.

There still is a serious stigma around veterans and PTSD. Although new laws have been passed and attention has been focused on the actual reasons for the diagnosis, as well as what the diagnosis is and is not, there is still a huge hill to climb. I have been unable to be employed, partly due to PTSD, and another part to migraines from several head injuries (yes from the military). I had volunteered many places but with all the limitations I had, it was always here and there. I volunteered mostly for the organizations my husband had a job with, much easier to tell him that I HAD to go and there not be any questions. It came to my attention that a veterans' resource center was to be established by a local mental health organization, Community Healthcore. I had tried to be involved with the veteran program they already had, but my inquires and application was continually not responded to. My contact seemed like she knew what she was doing. I had been to their training, had given her copies of my books to show that I knew what I was talking about, that I not only knew but had been there, just wanted to help in some way. Finally, I saw some information and called the number and it was the same person, Lori, that I had for months offering my help, but nothing.

I applied to be a volunteer but was eventually hired because the application for being a volunteer was taking longer than the process to be hired (I still think the volunteer application is sitting in some file folder). I thought it was a great pairing, I was hired as a peer mentor, with emphasis on consulting for VA programs, benefits, and other information that I brought to the table. I even pushed my husband to take a cut in pay and join me to help out other veterans. Once he did I had to be moved to another position so that we did not have the same supervisor. I was put under the same person (on paper only), Lori, that had done nothing with my volunteer application (for over a year then). At first she acted like I was the "everything," and she boasted about me often, well often in front of me. But once I moved over and brought my same work ethic to "her program," that is when everything changed.

She horded information I need to do my job, lied about numbers of veterans which were served, tried to blame me for not doing what she said she was going to do, lied to veterans, lied to veterans organization, did not know what she was doing, and had been doing nothing, well doing not much of anything, for years; all under the state funding program specifically to "help veterans." Veterans were coming in complaining about information she had given them which was totally wrong. Local veterans' organizations were not wanting to do anything if she was involved. She would not allow the promotional products (bouncy balls, pens, etc.) out to "just anyone," and that "just anyone" meant certain kinds of veterans. I could not understand how she still had the job.

There was something off about her and I could feel it. It was that feeling you do not understand, it does not fit in with the situation, but it was there. I made my feelings known and was told that it was probably just me, my inability to trust others, my PTSD issues. I thought myself out of my own feelings, figuring she just reminded me of someone, or something, but whatever that was, this was now, and I needed to move forward, typical therapy talk.

But I was done, even if it was me, I could not work this way, and there were other reasons beyond the feelings that I could easily point to. I complained and was told that I needed to just give her time, she had issues. She had issues? Here I was, the one who could not work full time, who was taking every precaution to not be triggered, the veteran and I was supposed to be patient with her? I asked to just be assigned something, I would take my part, and she could have everything else. That was the deal I made with her supervisor, who was really also mine. He made it seem as though he had made the decision and I had a task. I could not be partnered with someone who had no problems lying to veterans to make themselves seem like they were helping, when all she was doing was giving them hope where she fully knew there was none. It continually boggled my mind as to why she had not been fired yet, she had been fired from her last job, which pretty much was the same job in another region with another non-profit (same state funded program to help veterans). Others in the office asked what she had on the supervisor to keep him from firing her, I wondered that too.

The specific job did not last long, soon I needed information that she was supposed to give it to me, nope, she lied and said she did not have it. She did not have information that was critical to our jobs? I continued on and was being asked to do more and more, above what I was hired for. I was happy to do it, it helped veterans and I was all in. So the jealous began, what I did not realize is how bad it was, how evil she was, and how low she would go.

It was in the afternoon and I was about to leave. She got a call and quickly came to my desk, a veteran who was coming over wanted to talk about benefits, would I stay? That was my weakness. If anyone wanted to talk benefits, I was there. So I said yes. The veteran arrived but did not come into the room, he sat in the chair outside the office. As she walked by my desk to escort him to a "private area" so that we could talk without disruption, she stated "oh, by the way, he's in crisis." The color went out of my face. This was a young veteran in crisis, which most likely meant it was issues from combat. I had been very open about having PTSD, my triggers with combat, not doing any type of counseling, talking, or such. I could talk one-on-one about MST, to women MST survivors. I could talk all day about benefits to any veteran, but this was different. I knew then what she had purposely set up. She knew I was the only combat veteran in the office, she knew that many combat veterans feel comfortable talking only with other combat veterans. She knew he was in crisis (suicidal, had not eaten in days, had just been banned from campus which would stop the GI Bill payments, his only income), she knew the office was not equipped for anyone in crisis. She knew she should have called the organization's crisis team (since I had only worked there for a month, I did not know all that Community Healthcore did, or all the services they provided). She knew she did not have the capability to help him, even though in the past (she boasted to me) she had taken veteran suicide calls and had been incorrectly introduced as a crisis counselor for other veterans, but said nothing and counseled with them. She knew she should never have told the person on the phone to send him over to our office. She did this because she knew that I would put aside my mental health to make sure this veteran did not walk out the door and end his life. And that was what I did. And of course the first thing he asked was if I was a veteran and had I ever been in combat, when I said yes, he let the gates open.

I ended up at the VA with the psychiatric nurse saying he did not think that I should go home, that I should be hospitalized. I, because of the past experiences with VA, was not about to be hospitalized, I would die first, or take him out, which ever I had to do. I had brought along my husband and he talked the guy out of it. I know if I had gone in I never would have come out. It was talked over, did she really intend this, maybe it was just me, so I allowed "professionals" to interpret my feelings. I went in tears, still keeping back most of what I knew was going to come, and told who I thought was the person in charge of the entire veterans section. He told me to tell her supervisor, which I did, and then nothing. I was very clear when I told them what was done. I was very clear about the crisis situation the veteran was in (who admitted to having tried suicide and that was his plan had he not been helped and listened to by me), I did not think I had to explain what had been done to me, all that was said was that he would look into it. I believed him, I believed he, as a veteran, would not allow this to happen on his watch, I did not understand he did not care.

I was trying to hold it together with added medications from the VA and past VA meds that I had not taken for a long time, but were still in my cabinet. Yes, I was self-medicating to almost numb. Again she used my own words to injure me, she knew what would get to me, she had read my books and knew the triggers. I quit. I knew she would continue to hurt me until I either quit or was hospitalized, and I believe she wanted the latter. I was very specific to Community Healthcore when I gave my professional opinion that she was a danger, a risk to the very lives of veterans in the community. Oh, I explained the suicide calls she took, what she did to me, the lies she continually told veterans and local veterans organizations, even that one organization said if she tried to attend their programs she would be escorted to the door. What I did not know was even though there were many people who wanted to help veterans within the organization, it was not big on the table. It was a small grant, it pretty much was not worth veteran's lives to have a real inquiry. All my emails and calls to people I thought would care that this had occurred and cared about veterans, ended in nothing. Finally I had to face the fact that even though this was a mental health organization, they cared less about the mental health of one of their employees and veterans in general. That is the only conclusion I can come to because I am home, finally getting out of that mental break (it took over a year), and she is still working there, and I am still hearing her name spoken in anger, here and there, about another veteran she lied to.

It was a hard lesson to learn, and it did close me off again to the public. I do not think I will ever, no, I know that I will never do that again. My main focus is writing, crying when no one can see me, taking the mental breaks that I need, and writing about what I can handle (at this time). Although she mainly used the triggers I have about combat against me, she also employed other tactics that are connected to my traumas from the assaults (and the responses I received then), personal information I never thought, when writing my books, would ever be used against me. I was so very wrong. Even though this happened to me, I would be behind any veteran who wanted to volunteer, or be employed to help other veterans. I ran into a malicious person, packed in what looked like a small sweet lady, who all she "wanted" to do was help veterans. I let others, professionals, tell me that my feelings were not valid, that it was just me misreading the situation, my PTSD symptoms. When you know there is something off, believe your instincts, and believe in yourself. I will never discount those instinctional gut feelings again.

7
FILING A CLAIM

Note: This information is to assist you along with the help of another person to develop your claim. It is not intended and should not be used as the only resource to file your disability claim. Policies change all the time, therefore, this information was the best of my ability at the time it was retrieved.

If you are still in the military, you need to report it. Keeping documentation is imperative in case any physical or mental conditions result from the incident(s). There are many channels of reporting. Going to the website, sapr.mil, will give you some information about the procedures and what should happen, but be aware there are numerous reports, even with the new procedures, that victims are not being cared for properly.

What does it mean to have a mental disability? The stigma associated with this can be extremely negative. Many would rather continue struggling along without help, especially if help means the label of some mental disorder. It can be very difficult, but you need to get past the depressive thoughts and negative stigmas linked with a diagnosis in order to receive appropriate aid. A person is not weak in seeking help, and not damaged or less of a person because of a diagnosis. Faulty thinking occurs when the fear of accepting there is something wrong overrides the actual pattern of symptoms which are disrupting your life. Seeking help and asking for aid is extremely courageous, difficult but courageous!

Before filing a claim, you will need to understand that this most likely will not be a painless, frustrationless journey. The VA claims process is as quick as a snail, assembled with errors and requires constant vigilance to muddle through. It is an adversary to all veterans, and really not intended to be very helpful. Many MST survivors get triggered continuously during the process, but it is not a reason to quit. There are many well-experienced and educated individuals (about the claim process) just waiting to walk with you through this. They, at times, can seem to be the only person who believes you, but they are not the only ones. There are thousands of veterans who have traveled down this same path, and it is extremely unadvisable for you to not utilize what others know and have learned.

To file a claim for disability compensation is actually a simple process. I suggest before filing, you request all your military records. There could be documentation in the records, which may assist you in remembering events, times, people and so forth. If you are active duty, get a copy of all your records, personnel and medical, prior to discharge, even if you are not considering a claim.

Through eBenefits Veterans can: apply for benefits, view their disability compensation claim status, access official military personnel documents (e.g., DD Form 214, Certificate of Release or Discharge from Active Duty), (*KYB*, 2014).

You can file the claim yourself, which is very unadvisable. You can file with the help of another, and/or seek the help from an accredited Veterans Service Officer (VSO), who typically works for a Veterans Service Organization. It is greatly recommended to have a VSO since there can possibly be a time where the VA sends off a letter stating they have not received evidence, and the time limit is expired causing you to start from the beginning, or some other process-slowing event. Having an accredited VSO is a backup for these kinds of problems since all accredited VSOs should document what they have sent and what has been received from the VA, on your behalf. A VSO is not a replacement to finding another veteran to help you through this process, using someone who has been down this path before is advisable.

VSOs have more than one client, and since they are qualified to help in all compensation cases, they might not be particularly well-educated in the specific details used to not further trigger you when filing for compensation for symptoms caused by experience(s) of MST. There is nothing wrong with not using the first VSO that you see. This claim is for you and you need to have someone who will be able to have the knowledge and experience to help you with it. Unfortunately, many have just allowed any VSO to help them, and once your initial case has been denied, it is a more lengthy process for appeals. There are veterans who have been in the process of battling the VA over their claim for years;

yet, had all their information been included in their initial claim file, along with the proper way to explain the evidence, they would have been awarded a disability percentage. I cannot stress too much the weight the initial claim carries. There are no short-cuts, and there is no such thing as too many resources.

If you have already filed a claim, do not request a copy of your records. This will seriously slow down, if not halt, the already too long process. You can however request to review your file at the VA Regional Office it has been sent to. Give yourself plenty of time to allow the VA Regional Office to first, find the individual who is responsible for the records, and for a thorough review. It is advisable to take along someone who can take notes while you go through the file. That way you will not be side-tracked when you notice that a mistake has been made. It is also recommended, prior to allowing the file to proceed to the evaluation point, to view the file, ensure all the records attached to the file are yours (yes mistakes happen and inside your records you could find someone else's information), correct any mistakes (like the merging of someone else's file), check that all information you have submitted is included, and then request a hard copy from the Regional Office. This will allow you to be able to have a hard copy but should not delay the process. Question the individual at the Regional Office if requesting the hard copy at that time will slow or halt the course of your claim. There has been contradictory information from different veterans and VSOs about the availability to obtain a hard copy at this time, so ask. To request an appointment with the VA Regional Office to view your C-file, call 1-800-827-1000.

To win your claim you need three elements: a diagnosis, nexus, and evidence.
1. **A diagnosis** of the disorder or disease.
It is best you have a diagnosis of the disorder or disease which you are claiming. The most effective would come from a competent medical authority on mental health issues; typically a psychiatrist or psychologist, who is either employed by the VA or contracted with them to provide that service, for mental health issues and a VA M.D. or specialist in the field for physical disability. A diagnosis from an outside psychologist/psychiatrist, your VA health care provider or another therapist will also work;

however depending on the licensure they hold or do not hold, it can be considered a recommended diagnosis.

Be aware any other diagnosis beside PTSD; Depression and/or Anxiety, (e.g. Borderline Personality Disorder, Adjustment Disorder) does not necessarily meet what would describe most MST survivors to be suffering from, and is not a cause and effect for the sexual trauma you lived through. Although your symptoms can reflect the other diagnoses, what is missing is the trauma aspect which caused such symptomologies and that is a huge difference between the disorders. You can suffer from any personality disorder without ever having experienced MST; they can be genetic or said to have developed prior to your enlistment. However, you cannot be diagnosed with PTSD without having experienced a life-threatening trauma.

2. **Nexus**, link to service.
The claimed diagnoses must be linked to a verifiable (stressor) incident. The incident must have been during your service. If the diagnosis is PTSD, it is best to have in your medical chart a statement from a VA psychologist, psychiatrist or a psychologist, psychiatrist that the VA had contracted with, confirming the claimed stressor is adequate to support the claimed diagnosis. You will need a letter confirming the nexus (link) of your symptoms to the diagnosis, from a competent medical/mental health authority. If not in your VA medical file, the letter should include a statement effectively, such as: after reviewing (your name)'s medical records it is my opinion, more likely than not, her (diagnosis), is a direct result of military sexual trauma she experienced while serving on active duty. Any mental disorder diagnosed from the symptoms of experiencing MST should not be considered pre-existing. If you have listed a diagnosis which was pre-existing you need to be very specific and cautious about how the experience of MST aggravated the condition.

Upon acceptance into the military you go through a battery of health tests, a review of your civilian medical records, and a minor or in-depth investigation depending on your security clearance. At the point of acceptance there is a presumption of sound condition you are in, unless it is documented in your records, or where evidence or medical judgment is such as to warrant a finding that the disease or injury existed before acceptance and enrollment. There is not a wavier for having criteria which would fit any active mental disorder - PTSD, Major Depression and/or any personality disorder, so at the time of acceptance it is presumed you did not have these conditions; therefore, it would be difficult to state the diagnosis is pre-military, especially when the qualifying trauma occurred on active duty. If **everyone** who experienced sexual trauma or any other trauma developed PTSD or any of the other mental disorder there would not need to be criteria other than "trauma." Just listing a trauma was experienced is not enough, there needs to be a link established between the trauma, the symptoms you have (and are listed by a therapist), and your military service.

Wartime Disability Compensation.
§ 1111. Presumption of sound condition.
For the purposes of section 1110 of this title, every veteran shall be taken to have been in sound condition when examined, accepted, and enrolled for service, except as to defects, infirmities, or disorders noted at the time of the examination, acceptance, and enrollment, or where clear and unmistakable evidence demonstrates that the injury or disease existed before acceptance and enrollment and was not aggravated by such service.

General Entitlement to Compensation.
§ 1132. Presumption of sound condition For the purposes of section 1131 of this title, every person employed in the active military, naval, or air service for six months or more shall be taken to have been in sound condition when examined, accepted and enrolled for service, except as to defects, infirmities, or disorders noted at the time of the examination, acceptance and enrollment, or where evidence or medical judgment is such as to warrant a finding that the disease or injury existed before acceptance and enrollment (www.access.gpo.gov).

It is not uncommon for a MST survivor to have been sexually assaulted prior to their military employment. A large percentage of civilian women are sexually assaulted prior to becoming adults, so it is not completely unusual that the MST has added further trauma (even though alone MST can be completely responsible). The two traumas need to be separated. Your compensation is for military service time only so if you have any prior abuse that should not be utilized. All prior abused or traumas show a risk for developing other mental health conditions and by using these prior experiences the VA could conclude the symptoms you are now experiencing are linked to the prior trauma(s) and that your military trauma (usually not documented), does not have the weighted evidence to establish a link. I know this is not necessarily logical, but then the VA is not logical.

3. **Evidence**.

You should first request copies of all your military records (medical plus personnel files), any civilian records from the time you entered and any VA records. You also need to know what is and what is not listed in them. Obtaining your records might seem simple, but be aware; there are different requests for just your medical records. There is inpatient, outpatient and mental health records, and all should be listed separately on the forms along with the time frame for those records.

There are two types of evidence, what is referred to as direct/primary evidence and then alternative evidence which is called - markers. Direct evidence would be formal official documents such as: police reports, rape kit paperwork, crime report, the perpetrator's conviction, and/or the investigator's files. Do not worry if you do not have any direct evidence, most assaults go unreported.

The strongest evidence is if it was listed in your Service Medical Records, which should describe how the injury occurred, if there were any residual effects and the treatment(s), which could have been annotated over a period of time. You can also submit buddy letters. Buddy Letters are letters from individuals which could have been eye witnesses to the injury(s), behavioral changes and/or someone you told the assault to, relatively close to its happening.

Many MST survivors never reported the assault/incident(s), or no recorded report was made. Do not be discouraged, there are many avenues for finding alternate evidence or markers. A marker is evidence of behaviors which can occur after having experienced

MST. Such behaviors can be: an extreme increase or decrease in performance evaluations; substance abuse; frequent visits to medical facilities with or without diagnosed problems; increase disrespect for military authority (Write-ups, Letter of Reprimands, Article 15, even AWOL); problems with civilian authorities (vandalism, intoxicated in public, and/or shop lifting); marital problems; relationship problems; frequent requests for leave; requests for change of duties, shifts, units, stations; and more. What you are trying to show is that your behavior changed after a certain time, this time being when the incident(s) occurred.

...VA knows that events involving personal assault or sexual trauma are not always officially reported. Therefore, VA has relaxed the evidentiary requirements and looks for "markers" (i.e., signs events or circumstances) that provide some indication that the traumatic event happened, such as:

- *Records from law enforcement authorities, rape crisis centers, mental health counseling centers, hospitals, or physicians.*
- *Pregnancy tests or tests for sexually transmitted diseases.*
- *Statements from family members, roommates, fellow Servicemembers, clergy members, or counselors.*
- *Request for transfer to another military duty assignment.*
- *Deterioration in work performance.*
- *Substance abuse.*
- *Episodes of depression, panic attacks, or anxiety without an identifiable cause.*
- *Unexplained economic or social behavioral changes.*
- *Relationship issues, such as divorce.*
- *Sexual dysfunction (benefits.va.gov, 2015).*

Your Statement in Support of Claim should include what type of person you were before the assault, the assault (harassment), and then what type of person you are after. You do not need to tell the whole story or go into detail about the incident but you should list as many of the pertinent facts as you can. These facts are: your unit's name; your unit's commander; who the attacker was; where it happened; around what time of year (if you do not remember go for around holidays or within a three month span); his rank; his unit; the relationship to you (as per your career or otherwise); if you reported it and mention the evidence you have included (or will be including in the file). Writing "I was sexually assaulted on or about..." and then go from there should be enough detail about the assault itself, unless there is something specific which happened and caused a physical injury which you sought medical attention for or was seen by another person; such as "During the sexual assault (or physical attack) he hit me in the face," and you have documentation from a clinic or otherwise to the effect that you came in with a red mark on your face or a black eye. The more linked evidence the better.

When requesting someone write a letter for you about the behavior changes or physical conditions/injuries they noticed, they should use "the information is accurate to the best of my ability." You might be able to describe in detail the days prior, the day of, or the days after your assault with details as if you were watching them again, but you need to remember it was traumatic to you, more than likely they were just a bunch of other days to someone else and they might not even remember that month you are speaking about. I have such vivid memories of a lot of incidents, places, people, and even statements which were said, but when I asked for a buddy letter I was shocked the person hardly remembered the location we were at let alone all that occurred.

There is a general rating formula for mental disorders the VA uses, somewhat like a checklist, to assign a percentage to the degree of disability you are suffering from. You need to be familiar with it so that you can make sure you list the evidence (your symptoms) which matches the percentage you are suffering at. If you are diagnosed with PTSD do not assume any of the criteria for your diagnosis will be relevant unless you state the severity of your symptoms. Just as listed below with the 0% rating, you could be awarded service-connected PTSD and it be rated at 0% because the information needed to grant a higher award was not listed in your records, (and you did not put them in your claims file).

It is very difficult for most to discuss what they suffer from on a daily basis, especially when they believe they should be able to handle these feelings. If you have suicidal thoughts, no matter if it was a week ago and the therapist asks how you are doing, do not reply with the automatic "I'm fine" or "okay." You need to say that although you do not have them at the time you did think about killing yourself a few (or more) times in the past few weeks. Make sure at every appointment you have with your Primary Care Physician and/or your therapist the symptoms which you have experienced between appointments, even if the thought of suicide was a fleeting thought, is documented. Many are afraid if they admit they had those types of thoughts, or have some flashbacks they perceived to be hallucinations; that they will be locked up in a psych ward. This is not the case and keeping the symptoms you are experiencing inside, toughing it out, will only hurt you in the end. Nobody will read your mind and the VA will NOT assume anything. Not only will disclosing the real problems you are having allow the therapist to help you manage or teach you a new coping skill but the evaluator will be able to make a better decision about your functionability, and thereby granting a more appropriate percentage of disability.

4.130 General Rating Formula for Mental Disorders:

100% - Total occupational and social impairment, due to such symptoms as: gross impairment in thought processes or communication; persistent delusions or hallucinations; grossly inappropriate behavior; persistent danger of hurting self or others; intermittent inability to perform activities of daily living (including maintenance of minimal personal hygiene); disorientation to time or place; memory loss for names of close relatives, own occupation, or own name.

70 % - Occupational and social impairment, with deficiencies in most areas, such as work, school, family relations, judgment, thinking, or mood, due to such symptoms as: suicidal ideation; obsessional rituals which interfere with routine activities; speech intermittently illogical, obscure, or irrelevant; near-continuous panic or depression affecting the ability to function independently, appropriately and effectively; impaired impulse control (such as unprovoked irritability with periods of violence); spatial disorientation; neglect of personal appearance and hygiene; difficulty in adapting to stressful circumstances (including work or a work-like setting); inability to establish and maintain effective relationships.

50% - Occupational and social impairment with reduced reliability and productivity due to such symptoms as: flattened affect; circumstantial, circumlocutory, or stereotyped speech; panic attacks more than once a week; difficulty in understanding complex commands; impairment of short- and long-term memory (e.g., retention of only highly learned material, forgetting to complete tasks); impaired judgment; impaired abstract thinking; disturbances of motivation and mood; difficulty in establishing and maintaining effective work and social relationships.

30 % - Occupational and social impairment with occasional decrease in work efficiency and intermittent periods of inability to perform occupational tasks (although generally functioning satisfactorily, with routine behavior, self-care, and conversation normal), due to such symptoms as: depressed mood, anxiety, suspiciousness, panic attacks (weekly or less often), chronic sleep impairment, mild memory loss (such as forgetting names, directions, recent events).

10% - Occupational and social impairment due to mild or transient symptoms which decrease work efficiency and ability to perform occupational tasks only during periods of significant stress, or; symptoms controlled by continuous medication.

0% - A mental condition has been formally diagnosed, but symptoms are not severe enough either to interfere with occupational and social functioning or to require continuous medication (http://www.benefits.va.gov).

Note in the listing above the 10% states symptoms controlled by continuous medications. This is to say that all of your symptoms are being controlled by medications and that the symptoms are not significantly disrupting your life. Read the ratings over again and make sure you understand all the implications.

Your C&P appointment.
Typically you will receive a C&P exam appointment. The time and/or date of the exam may be inconvenient but you need to keep this appointment if at all possible. If you know there is a conflict then as soon as you are aware of the appointment call and change

it, do not wait even a day. Be on time or early for the appointment. If you show up late, depending on how late you are, it can be considered a "no show" and that is a huge negative mark.

Understand the C&P exam is going to be terrible. You are going to be asked questions which the answers you may have never discussed with anyone. These questions, to the VA, are necessary to determine the legitimacy of your claim and the degree of disability you are suffering from. The questions are not purposely designed to trigger you, the examiner is not trying to be mean, but these things do happen. It is not recommended that you go to this appointment alone. You will already be tightly wound so getting into the driver's seat is wrong and hazardous. You should have someone who has been supportive go with you, and even go in to the exam (this depends on your approval only, not another's, if you do not want them in the exam then they need to stay out). It can be extremely helpful for your husband or wife to accompany you; lend support, be another source of memories and a witness to the behaviors you have been exhibiting.

Try to keep yourself grounded and in the present during the exam. While you are sitting in the waiting room do not allow yourself to obsess over what the exam will be like and/or what the questions will be; have a bunch of comic strips you have collected or a funny book or watch videos (with headphones on so that no one else can hear) that can occupy your mind and help you laugh inside. You can use breathing techniques, quick memory joggers, imagery, note taking, doodling or even have a Battle Buddy with you. A Battle Buddy is my own design, a small pocket animal carrying a rucksack with a pleasant aroma, designed to calm you and encompasses three of your senses: touch; sight; and especially smell (if you like adding a crinkle in the pack engages hearing also). I have tried the worry stone. Sure there was a positive word carved into it, and even though when I rubbed it, it did get hot, in the end it was just a rock. So I thought about the times that I was at my lowest, what helped me through it, and it dawned on me, Killer had. I held him, rubbed his fur, and that soft fur, his eyes, with my prayers brought a smile to my face, at the darkest of times. I researched what would engage most of my senses, and that is what I came up with. It is a type of therapy for me to make them, and I know they head off to help others. Yes, it is a little "stuffed animal" (small to fit in the pocket), but my "fluffy puppy" (what I called Killer) would rip you apart before allowing any harm to come to me. That is what I feel as I hold mine, that feel of unconditional love. **(Order your Battle Buddy at www.wells2000llc.com\battlebuddy).**

The examiner is going to judge you; it is her/his job. They are going to take into account: how you are dressed; how is your hygiene; the manner in which you answer questions; your affect; if you were on time; how often you needed the questions repeated; if your answers are relevant to the questions; how long it takes you to respond; and other observable aspects. Try to stay composed (yes I understand it will be challenging). Be honest, when asked questions like "how are you doing today" we tend to give the automatic reply "I'm fine." You are not fine; if you were fine you would not be there. Even if you have no emotional responses talking about the trauma (numbing) that is definitely still not fine. It is normal and natural for you to be anxious, scared, jumpy, worried and on the edge of your seat. You probably did not get any sleep the night before, you may not have been able to get a full night sleep for a very long time, and this is totally understandable. So say "I couldn't sleep last night and I really cannot remember the last time I got a full night's sleep."

For simplicity, when asked questions about your moods and behavior pick a day or two, in the last 90 days, that was your worst day(s) and respond to the questions with them in mind. It will allow your thoughts to not begin to contradict one another, and it should lengthen your ability to stay focused. Preferably you need to stay with facts that have documentation to back them up. Freely offer information if you see the line of questioning heading that way; this is not an interrogation. Do not assume the examiner can read your mind and will of course infer something helpful to your case, when you have not said it; she/he will not. Their interpretation can be the opposite of what you are feeling, but if you do not tell them, they will make their own judgement call.

The examiner has a short amount of time so do not take it up with stories about how bad you have been treated by the VA; how difficult it has been to gather all the evidence; your negative experience(s) with some VSOs; how complicated and adversarial the process is; and/or how the process after the exam will go. This is the time to make your case and wasting this time will cost only you in the long run. The examiner should not ask you to describe the assault in detail, and if he/she does you do not have to disclose that information, and I would advise against it. The same simple statement you placed on the claims form is enough. This exam is not to retraumatize you; it is to determine if you have a service connected disability. The appointment is going to be traumatic on its own without the possibility of triggering you into more severe symptoms. There will be many who work with veterans who will disagree with you not telling the entire story, but from my own experience and the experience I personally know of hundreds of others, the detailed information is not needed for the claim and in the end only will hurt you. Stating "I just can't talk about it" or "I don't want to talk about the specifics," should be enough detail for the evaluator.

Even after all you do, and all the evidence you have submitted, you may receive a denial letter. For many survivors this is just another slap in the face, almost saying "you lied and we do not believe you." Know that this is not what is being said. A denial to the claim is not a denial the assault happened, that you are not suffering, or that you do not have a mental illness. The denial can merely be that: one small box was not checked, a simple missed word, a misunderstanding of the terms an outside source used, any number of reasons; I know it will not help, but try not to take the denial personally, it is not another purposeful attack to just you. I have seen hundreds of denials where there was only missing some small annotation. Denial letters are not personal attacks, most of the ones that I have view are just wide-spread strike to all survivors in general. After your initial denial or award, you can fight if you believe the rating was incorrect, but it is better to go through that process (fighting the incorrect rating) than giving up and dealing on your own.

The VA does not put in counselors to help the veteran immediately following the C&P appointment, the C&P is not therapy. The C&P is not about the "what" of the details that happened but the "how" it effects you today (symptoms).

When answering questions about your symptoms, be specific, direct, truthful to the best of your ability and if you do not know the answer say so. This is not an exam where there a specific correct answer to every question. The correct answer is the truth; and "I do not know" can be the truth. Always be polite, do not yell and do not swear. You want the examiner to remember you in a positive light, not someone who had angry outbursts and chose to degrade yourself and the examiner with such language, if it can be controlled.

These are suggestions for when you have your exam, however you can utilize any of them for any of your other VA appointments also:

- Prior to the appointment pick a spot where you can go after the exam and be just with the person who brought you. Numerous veterans have exited the exam to go sit in their car and breakdown into tears for some time.
- This is not a job interview, do not dress up. Look as close as you can to one of your bad days. And I do mean no make-up, frumpy clothes, hair not brushed, like one of the bad days.
- Do not schedule any other appointments that day or the next few days (unless it is a therapy appointment) because you will need this break to absorb what you just went through.
- Make sure you let your therapist know about this appointment and have a plan set before-hand to contact her/him in case of emergency.
- Make sure you are not alone for awhile. You might feel like you want everyone to go away but at this sensitive time it is not good to be by yourself.
- Be nice to yourself, replaying the exam in your mind to see where you assume you were not clear enough or were not understood is not healthy and will not do any good.
- Prior to the day of the exam prepare small meals you can freeze so that food will not have to be a long thought out process, or decide take out is the menu.
- When you get home take a long bubble, salt, or essential oil bath, or if you prefer a long hot shower.
- Have your favorite funny movie or clips waiting.

- Allow others to take care of you. This is not a time to play super mom/wife/friend; and by the way there is a reason you see them in comic books – they are not real.
- If you are working take vacation/sick days around that time.
- Get take-out and eat in.
- If you have small children see if a family member or friend can take care of them if it will help. Other veterans like to come home to see their family and be surrounded with the ones who support and love them; do whatever you believe will be best.
- If you have teenagers make it known this is not a day to discuss anything or to be asked anything…mom is off duty.
- Write down your plan for that day. Do not rely on your memory; your brain has already worked overtime.

This is just a small list; you should brainstorm what would be the best for you, all before the day of the exam but keep it simple. Share this list with the person who will go with you or someone who will be with you after so that you will have a supporter to keep you on track.

If you have accomplished all the above then it is time to just wait. Writing the VA nasty letters venting about the slowness of the process and how long your case is taking will not move your case forward. If you do need to contact the VA over your case it should be in a very simple formatted letter and for a specific reason, not to see how the case is coming or when they believe you might get a decision. Letters will be sent out occasionally stating your claim is being worked on, even though they are the same form letters with just different dates. Now you can access on ebenefits.va.gov the status of your claim, it will be vague.

There are six basic phases of an appeal:
- **Appeal Pending**: You have initiated an appeal, but at this point your case is still with the local VA office that made the decision on your case. If you have questions about your appeal, please contact that office or your representative, if you have one.
- **Administrative Case Processing**: After BVA receives your case, it is processed and stored in a secure location until it is assigned to a Veterans Law Judge (VLJ) based on your

docket number, which identifies your place in the line of cases to be decided by BVA.

- **With VSO**: This indicates that your Veterans Service Organization (VSO) representative has your claims file for review.
- **With VLJ**: This indicates that a Veterans Law Judge has your claims file and will take appropriate action on your appeal.
- **Pending Dispatch**: This indicates that the Veterans Law Judge made a decision on your appeal, and that BVA will mail the decision to you soon.
- **Decision & Claims File Dispatch**: This indicates that BVA mailed the decision to you (and your representative, if any) and transferred your case to another location. Please refer to your Appeal Detail screen for further information about the specific location of your case.

Some Extra tips. Make sure…
- Get a notebook (spiral is good) and file folder. Keep detailed records of when you communicate with your VSO and the VA. You should annotate every call, letter, and appointment, with dates, times, what was talked about and who was talked to.
- If sending anything to the VA directly do not use a fax, an email, regular mail or even hand delivering it; only use certified mail, a VSO, or ebenfits. This allows you to show they did receive a letter and when it was received.
- Attach the certified mail slip to a copy of the letter then place it in your file, chronologically; it helps if there is a question about something sent a few months back.
- Always send copies, **Never** send the originals (**to anyone**). If for some reason the mail does not make it then you could have lost a valuable piece of your claim.
- Keep all correspondences sent to you from individuals, your VSO, the VA and any other organization you have contacted in regard to your claim.
- Understand not everyone at the VA will know the information you are asking for. Also you can receive incorrect information from VA staff.
- Do not be afraid to ask questions.

- If you feel awkward or unsettled after speaking with anyone, do not let it go by, tell someone.
- Always describe what your symptoms really are and how they are really affecting you, even if you feel embarrassed. Down-playing the symptoms because you are afraid of judgments will only hurt you in the end. If for the past week you did not get out of bed to even take a shower, have it annotated on your records.
- Accept help, from an experienced and educated person (about the claim process) with your claim.
- When sending in documents (evidence) use the VA forms. Keep a copy of all the letters you send.
- Do not be afraid to complain if something wrong does happen.
- If you are not comfortable with a male health care provider, you can request a woman. I now will only use a woman Primary Care Physician, a woman nurse, and a woman therapist.

Keep all appointments. If an emergency arises and you absolutely cannot make the appointment CALL and reschedule. Never allow a missed appointment on your VA records.

8
VETERANS ADMINISTRATION

Many women veterans believe they are not "veterans" if they have not served in a combat zone, this is completely untrue. You are a veteran!

The Veterans Health Administration (VHA), within the Department of Veterans Affairs (VA), operates the nation's largest integrated direct health care delivery system, provides care to approximately 5.75 million unique veteran patients, and employs more than 270,000 full-time equivalent employees. While Medicare, Medicaid, and the Children's Health Insurance Program (CHIP) are also publicly funded programs, most health care services under these programs are delivered by private providers in private facilities. In contrast, the VA health care system could be categorized as a veteran-specific national health care system, in the sense that the federal government owns the medical facilities and employs the health care providers.

The VA offers all enrolled veterans a standard medical benefits package that includes (among other things) inpatient care, outpatient care, and prescription drugs. The VA's standard medical benefits package includes a broad spectrum of inpatient, outpatient, and preventive medical services, such as the following:
- medical, surgical, and mental health care, including care for substance abuse;
- prescription drugs, including over-the-counter drugs, and medical and surgical supplies available under the VA national formulary system;
- durable medical equipment and prosthetic and orthotic devices, including hearing aids and eyeglasses (subject to limitations);
- home health services, hospice care, palliative care, and institutional respite care;
- noninstitutional adult day health care and noninstitutional respite care; and
- periodic medical exams, among other services (Panangla, 2014).

The VA is divided into VISNs, Veterans Integrated Service Networks. There are 23 networks across the United States, Virgin Islands, Puerto Rico, Philippines Islands, and Guam.

"General Eligibility: Eligibly for most VA benefits is based upon discharge from active military service under other than dishonorable conditions. Active service means full-time service, other than active duty for training, as a member of the Army, Navy, Air Force, Marines Corps, Coast Guard…

Dishonorable and bad conduct discharges issued by general courts-martial may bar VA benefits. Veterans in prison must contact VA to determine eligibility. VA benefits will not be provided to any Veteran or dependent wanted for an outstanding felony warrant" (DoD, *Know Your Benefits*, 2014).

The VA places each Veteran is to an assigned priority group based on specific criteria. The VA uses these groups to balance the demand for resources and health care. There can be changes which occur that limit access to care for specific groups, when the demand increases over the resources available. The VA has stated if this occurs there will be a public notification and the affected enrollees will be contacted.

ebenefits is a joint VA/Department of Defense (DoD) Web portal that provides resources and self-service capabilities to Servicemembers, Veterans, and their families to apply, research, access, and manage their VA and military benefits and personal information through a secure Internet connection (*KYB*, 2014).

Military Sexual Trauma is determined by the statement of the veteran declaring they experienced MST. Eligibility for services is determined by the VA clinician who decides which problems are related to the MST, other than therapy. Although receiving counseling and/or medical care for problems associated with MST can be thought as admirable from the VA. If you are not granted service-connected status, a medical clinician will establish what is and is not connect to the MST. Filing a claim for Posttraumatic Stress Disorder, Major Depression and/or Anxiety (symptomology from typical Military Sexual Trauma experience) because of symptoms which interfere with your life is not a "hand out." The compensation is not a gift, it is what you deserve. Many MST survivors struggle over being labeled as disabled or having a mental disorder, thereby not receiving their rightful benefits. When you joined the military, you signed a contract which bound you and the government. You held up your side, it is now time for the government to hold up theirs.

VA provides readjustment and counseling services, to include direct counseling, outreach, and referral, through 300 community-based Vet Centers located in all 50 states, the District of Columbia, GUAM, Puerto Rico, and American Samoa.

Eligibility: Veterans and active-duty Servicemembers, to include federally-activated members of the National Guard and Reserve components, are eligible to receive readjustment counseling services at a Vet Center if they:

1. Have served on active military duty in any combat theater or area of hostility such as World War II, the Korean War, the Vietnam War, the Gulf War, or the campaigns in Lebanon, Grenada, Panama, Somalia, Bosnia, Kosovo, Afghanistan, and Iraq;
2. Experienced a military sexual trauma while servicing on active duty;
3. Provided direct emergent medical care or mortuary services, while serving active military duty, to the casualties of war;
4. Served as a member of an unmanned aerial vehicle crew that provided direct support to operations in a combat zone or area of hostility; or
5. Are Veterans who served in the active military during the Vietnam-era, but not in the Republic of Vietnam, and have requested services at a Vet Center before January 1, 2004.

Vet Center readjustment counseling services are free to the eligible Veterans and their family without time limitations. Servicemembers and Veterans are not required to enroll in the VA health care system or have received a service connection for conditions caused by military service. These services are also provided regardless of the nature of the Veteran's discharge. This includes service provision to those individuals with problematic discharges.

Services Offered: Vet Centers counselors provide individual, group, marriage, and family readjustment counseling to those individuals that have served in combat zones or areas of hostilities to assist them in making a successful transition from military to civilian life; to include treatment for posttraumatic stress disorder (PTSD) and help with any other military related problems that affect functioning within the family, work, school or other areas of everyday life. Other psycho-social services include outreach, education, medical referral, homeless Veteran services, employment, VA benefit referral, and the brokering of non-VA services (DOD, *Know Your Benefits*, 2014).

Whether or not you have decided to file a claim for compensation and/or pension at this time, you should obtain a copy of all your military records. There are two types of records: 1) Individual Health and Service Records and 2) Clinical Records. Clinical records are inpatient records filed by the military hospital or other medical facility which provided treatment to you. A summary of your treatment can be listed in your Service Medical Records (SMRs) but does not usually include all the hospital notes and tests. Most of the Official Military Personnel Files contained both personnel and active duty health records but that was discontinued in 1992 where the medical records are now separate and filed with the Veteran's Administration, and the Official Military Personnel Files (OMPFs) are kept at the National Archives and Records Administration's National Personnel Records Center, Military Personnel Records (NARA-NPRC-MPR) - if you have been discharged at least 6 months with no reserve obligation (active or inactive).

You should keep copies of all your records together and in a fire-proof container. It is not uncommon for records to be misplaced, lost, or become non-existent even when there is proof they once existed. If you are still in the military, you need to obtain a copy of all your records prior to your discharge. This is a back-up in case there comes a time when a condition arises or worsens because of your service and/or you need your files to prove some part of your enlistment (duty assignments, duty stations, TDYs, etc.).

Complaints

Occasionally you might come across a time in which you need to file a complaint. There are many, who do not like to cause problems, but you are not the cause of the problem and if you allow what has happened to go without documentation then another veteran, or yourself, could suffer. You do not have to accept any medical procedures, and you have a right to refuse them.

The VA (is supposed to) tracks all the complaints which are made. However, sometimes just stating something is wrong is not enough, and you need to put into writing what is occurring or the incident which happened. This is not whining, many of us veterans cannot afford, or cannot get insurance outside of the VA so it is your duty as a fellow veteran to make sure if there is a problem that the problem is address and handled to help us all.

VHA Patient Advocacy Program
A **complaint** is a gap between service expectations and actual experience. A complaint may be expressed verbally or in writing to any employee as well as to officials outside of the facility, such as congressional officers or veteran service officers.

A **Facility or Medical Center Patient Advocate** is an employee who is specifically designated at each VHA facility to manage the complaint process, including complaint resolution, data capture and analysis of issues/complaints in order to make system improvements. Facility or Medical Center Patient Advocates assist front-line staff in resolving issues that occur at the point of service and address complaints that were not able to be resolved at the point of service. Facility or Medical Center Patient Advocates work directly with Service Chiefs and Service management to facilitate resolution to problems beyond the scope of front-line staff, and participate in resolution of system problems by presenting the patient's perspective of the problem and desired resolution.

Inquiry Routing and Information System (IRIS) allows veterans to submit questions, complaints, compliments and suggestions through the VA website. The veteran self-directs inquiries, which are routed to the appropriate VA Central Office Program Offices, Network or facility, where care was provided. The preferred method of electronic communication for VHA with its constituents is through the use of IRIS (iris.va.gov).

Resources

afpc.af.mil/library/sapr/index.asp
afterdeployment.org
centerfotthestudyoftraumaticstress.org
cnic.navy.mil
hadit.com
healingcombattrauma.org
healthquality.va.gov/ptsd
icisf.org
insidemilitarysexualtrauma.blogspot.com
istss.org
maketheconnection.net/conditions/military-sexual-trauma
mentalhealth.va.gov/msthome.asp
military.com
militaryonesource.mil
myduty.mil
nationalguard.mil/jointstaff/j1/sapr
nimh.nih.gov
nlm.nih.gov/medlineplus/depression.html
ptsd.va.gov
safehelpline.org
sapr.mil
samhsa.gov
sexualassault.army.mil
uscg.mil/sapr/sapr_glossary.asp
usmc-mccs.org/sapro
va.gov
vawatchdog.org
vetcenter.va.gov
womenshealth.va.gov/womenshealth/trauma.asp

9
ACRONYMS/ABBREVIATIONS

38 USC - Title 38 of the United States Code
AD - Active Duty
AF – Air Force
AFB – Air Force Base
AFOSI – Air Force Office of Special Investigations
AL – American Legion
AMVETS - AMVETS (American Veterans)
AO - Agent Orange
AWOL – Absent With Out Leave
BCD - Bad Conduct Discharge
BPD – Borderline Personality Disorder
BVA - Board of Veterans Appeals
CAVC - Court of Appeals for Veterans Claims
CBOC – Community Based Outpatient Clinic
CBT – Cognitive Behavior Therapy
C-File - Claims File
C&P – Compensation and Pension
CID – Criminal Investigation Division
CUE - Clear and Unmistakable Error
DAV – Disabled American Veterans
DD - Dishonorable Discharge
DD-214 - Certificate of Release or Discharge from Active Duty
DoD - Department of Defense
DRB - Discharge Review Board
DRO - Decision Review Officer
DSM-IV - Diagnostic and Statistical Manual of Mental Disorders 4th Edition
DSM-V - Diagnostic and Statistical Manual of Mental Disorders 5th Edition
DTAP – Disabled Veterans' Transition Assistance Program
DV – Disabled Veteran
EEO - Office of Equal Opportunity
FY – Fiscal Year
GAF - Global Assessment of Function
HCP – Healthcare Personnel
HVRP - Homeless Veterans' Reintegration Program
IRIS - Inquiry Routing and Information System
I/U - Individual Unemployabilty
JAG – Judge Advocates General
MCIO – Military Criminal Investigative Organizations
MST – Military Sexual Trauma
NAVA – National Organization for Victim Assistance
NCIS – Navy Criminal Investigative Service
NSO - National Service Officer
NSVRC – National Sexual Violence Resource Center
NVLSP - National Veterans Legal Services Program
OEF – Operation Enduring Freedom
OIF – Operation Iraqi Freedom
P&T - Permanently and Totally Disabled
PCT – PTSD Clinic Team
PL – Public Law
PRRP – PTSD Residential Treatment Program
PTSD – Post-Traumatic Stress Disorder

PTSD Dom – PTSD Domiciliary
PVA - Paralyzed Veterans of America
SAFE – Sexual Assault Forensic Examination
SAPR – Sexual Assault Prevention and Response Program
SAPRO – Sexual Assault Prevention and Response Office
SARCs – Sexual Assault Response Coordinators
SC - Service Connected
SIPP – Specialized Intensive PTSD Program
SIPU – Specialized Inpatient PTSD Unit
SMR – Service Medical Records
SO - Service Officer
SOC - Statement of the Case
SOPP – Specialized Outpatient PTSD Program
SUPT – Substance Use PTSD Team
TAP – Transition Assistance Program
TBI – Traumatic Brain Injury
UCMJ – Uniform Code of Military Justice
USAF – United States Air Force
USMC – United States Marine Corps
USN – United States Navy
VA – Department of Veterans Affairs
VAMC – Veterans Administration Medical Center
VARO –Veteran's Administration Regional Office
VAs – Victim Advocates
VFW - Veterans of Foreign Wars of the United States.
VSO – Veterans Service Organization
WSDTT – Women's Stress Disorder Treatment Team
WTRP – Women's Trauma Recovery Program

10
REFERENCES

1.va.gov/womenvet/page.

Air Force Recruiting Service Instruction 36-2001. (2012). http://static.e-publishing.af.mil/production/1/afrs/publication/afrsi36-2001/afrsi36-2001.pdf. Retrieved Mar 2015.

Airforce.com/learn-about/our-mission/. Retrieved Mar 2015.

American Psychiatric Association. (2000). *.Diagnostic and statistical manual of mental disorders*, (4th ed., Rev. ed.). Washington, DC.: American Psychiatric Association.

American Psychiatric Association. (2012). *DSM.* psycg.org/practice/dsm.

Army Regulations 600-20. (2008).

Barrett, D.H., Doebbeling, C.C., Schwartz, D.A., et al. (2002). Posttraumatic stress disorder and self-reported physical health status among U.S. military personnel serving during the gulf war period. *Psychosomatics, 43* (3), 195-205.

Butterfield, M., McIntyre, L., Stechuchak, K., Nanda, K., & Bastian, L. (1998). Mental disorder symptoms in veteran women: Impact of physical and sexual assault. *Journal of the American Medical Women's Association, 53*, 198-200.

Campbell, R., & Raja, S. (2005). The sexual assault and secondary victimization of female veterans: Help-seeking experiences with military and civilian social systems. *Psychology of Women Quarterly, 29,* 97-106.

Clum, G.A., Calhoun, K., & Kimmerling, R. (2000). Associations among symptoms of depression and posttraumatic stress disorder and self-reported health in sexually assaulted women. *The Journal of Nervous and mental Disease, 188* (10), 671-678.

Committee on Treatment of Posttraumatic Stress Disorder. (2007) *Treatment of posttraumatic stress disorder: An assessment of the evidence.* (uncorrected proofs). The National Academies Press.

Coyle, B.S., Wolan, D. L., & Van Horn, A. S. (1996). The prevalence of physical and sexual abuse in women veterans seeking care at a Veterans Affairs medical center. *Military Medicine, 161*, 588-593.

Davis, T., & Wood, P. (1999). Substance abuse and sexual trauma in female veteran population. *Journal of Substance Abuse Treatment, 16* (2), 123-127.

Defense Research, Surveys, and Statistics Center (RSSC). *2014 Survivor Experience Survey, Report on Preliminary Results, FY 2014, Quarter 4.* dtic.mil/dtic (report No. 2014-037). Retrieved Apr 2015.

Department of Veterans Affairs. (2004). *Military sexual trauma* (Independent Study Course).

Department of Veterans Affairs. (2009). *The center for women veterans: Counseling & medical treatment for the after affects of sexual trauma.* www.va.gov.

Department of Veterans Affairs. (2014). *Federal benefits for veterans dependents & survivors*. U.S. Government Printing Office.

Department of Veterans Affairs. (2013). *Disability compensation military sexual trauma (MST)*. benefits.va.gov/benefits/factsheets/serviceconnected /mst.pdf. Retrieved Dec, 2013.

Department of Veterans Affairs. National Center for PTSD. *PTSD treatment programs in the U.S. department of Veterans Affairs*. ptsd.va.gov/public. Retrieved Oct, 2010.

Finn, Peter, (1995). *Preventing Alcohol-Related Problems on Campus: Acquaintance rape*. Higher Education Center for Alcohol and Other Drug Prevention. Abt Associates Inc. edc.org/hec/. Retrieved Mar 2015.

Fischer, L.A. (1999). *Ultimate power: Enemy within the ranks*. Hawaii: Unlimited Inc.

FY 2013 DoD Annual Report on Sexual Assault in the military. (2014). sapr.mil/public/docs/reports/FY13_DoD_SAPRO_Annual_on_Sexual_Assault.pdf. Retrieved Mar 2015.

Himmelfarb, N., Yaeger, D., & Mintz, J. (2006). Posttraumatic stress disorder in female veterans with military and civilian sexual trauma. *Journal of Traumatic Stress, 19* (6), 837-846.

Hoge, C.W., Castro, C.A., Messer, S.C., McGurk, D. Cotting, D.I., & Koffman, R.L. (2004). Combat duty in Iraq and Afghanistan, mental health problems, and barriers to care. *New England Journal of Medicine, 351*, 13-22.

Hyun, J.K., Pavao, J., & Kimerling, R. (2009) Military sexual trauma. *PTSD Research Quarterly: Advancing Science and Promoting Understanding of Traumatic Stress, 20* (2).

Johnson, L.A. (1993, February). Hidden agony. *Tambuli*, 27. lds.org/ldsorg/v/index.jsp?hideNav. Retrieved Oct, 2010.

Karp, S.A., Silber, D.E., Holmstrom, R.W., & Stock, L.J. (1995). Personality of rape survivors as a group and by relation of survivor to perpetrator. *Journal of Clinical Psychology, 51*, 587.

Kasper, P., & White, R. *Help with your VA claims*. mrfa.org/VA.Claim.htm. Retrieved Oct, 2010.

Kessler, R., Sonnega, A., Bromet, E., Hughes, M., & Nelson, C. (1995). Posttraumatic stress disorder in the national comorbidity survey. *Archives of General Psychiatry, 52*, 1048-1060.

Kimerling, R., Gima, K., Smith, M.W., Street, A., & Frayne, S. (2007). The veterans health administration and military sexual trauma. *American Journal of Public Health, 97* (12).

King, D.W., King, L.A., & Vogt, D.S. (2003) *Manual for the deployment risk and resilience inventory (DRRI): A collection of measures for studying deployment-related experiences of military veterans*. Boston: National Center for PTSD.

LaMar, W.J., Gerberich, S.G., Lohman, W.H., & Zaidman, B. (1998). Work-related physical assault. *Journal of Occupational Environmental Medicine, 40,* 317-324.

Marines.com/history-heritage/our-purpose. Retrieved Mar 2015.

Martin, L., Rosen, L., Durand, D., Kundson, K., & Stretch, R. (2000). Psychological and physical health effects of sexual assaults and nonsexual trauma among male and female United States Army soldiers. *Behavior Medicine, 26,* 23-34.

Murdoch, M., & Nichol, K.L. (1995). Women veterans' experiences with domestic violence and with sexual harassment while in the military. *Archives of Family Medicine, 4,* 411-418.

National Defense Authorization Act for Fiscal Year 2013, gpo.gov/fdsys/pkg/BILLS-112hr4310enr/pdf/BILLS-112hr4310enr.pdf. Retrieved Mar 2015.

National Institute of Justice Centers for Disease Control and Prevention. (1998). *Prevalence, incidence, and consequences of violence against women: findings from the National violence against women survey.* Washington, DC.: U.S. Department of Justice.

Navy.com/about/mission.html. Retrieved Mar 2015.

Panagla, S., Bagalman, E., 92014). *Health Care for Veterans: Answers to Frequently Asked Questions.* Congressional Research Service, (7-5700). crs.gov R42747. Retrieved Apr, 2015.

Pritt, A.F. (2001, April). Healing the spiritual wounds of sexual abuse. *Ensign ,58.* Retrieved October, 2010, from: lds.org/ldsorg/v/index.jsp?hideNav.

Powers, Rod. (2015). *Military Criminal History (Moral) Waivers.* http://usmilitary.about.com/od/joiningthemilitary/a/moralwaivers.htm, Retrieved Mar, 2015.

Sadler, A.G., Booth, B.M., Cook, B.L., & Doebbeling, B.N. (2003). Factors associated with women's risk of rape in the military environment. *American Journal of Industrial Medicine, 43,* 262-273.

Sadler, A.G., Booth, B.M., Cook, B.L., Torner, J.C., & Doebbeling, B.N. (2001). The military environment: Risk factors for women's non-fatal assaults. *Journal of Occupational and Environmental Medicine, 43* (4), 325-334.

Sadler, A.G., Booth, B., Nielson, D., & Doebbeling, B. (2000). Health-related consequences of physical and sexual violence: Women in the military. *Obstetrics & Gynecology, 96,* 473-480.

Sampson, Rana (2002). *Guide No. 17: Acquaintance Rape of College Students.* popcenter.org/problems/rape/1. Retrieved Mar 2015.

Valente, S., & Wight, C. (2007). Military sexual trauma: Violence and sexual abuse. *Military Medicine, 172* (3), 259-265.

Veterans Administration. *General rating formula for mental disorders.* Retrieved October 2010, from: benefits.va.gov/warms/docs/regs/38CFR/BOOKC/PART4/S4_130.DOC.

Veterans Health Administraion. *Military sexual trauma (MST) programming.* Retrieved October 2010, from: 1.va.gov/vhapublications.

Vogt, D., Monson, C., Resick, P., & Welch, L. *PTSD 101: Sexual assault and PTSD*. Retrieved February 2009, from: ncptsd.va.gov/ptsd101.

Walker, M. (2007). *Crossing the blue code*. Nebraska: iuniverse.

Walker, M. (2008). *Beyond the blue code*. Nebraska: iuniverse.

Yaegar, D., Himmelfarb, N., Cammack, A., & Mintz, J. (2006). DSM-IV diagnosed posttraumatic stress disorder in women veterans with and without military sexual trauma. *Journal of General internal Medicine, 21*, S65-S69.

Zinzow, H., Grubaugh, A., Monnier, J., Suffoletta-Malerie, S., & Freuh, B. (2007). Trauma among female veterans: A critical review. *Trauma, Violence, & Abuse, 8*, 384-400.